ABOUT *THE COMPASSIONATE WARRIOR: ABD EL-KADER OF ALGERIA*

"This clear and accessible biography will provide young readers with a valuable portrait of the Emir Abd el-Kader, who was so admired in 19th-century America. It is an admirable contribution to the understanding of the encounters between Muslims and Christians in the age of colonialism."

—**Carl W. Ernst**, University of North Carolina at Chapel Hill, author of *How to Read the Qur'an: A New Guide, with Select Translations* and editor of *Islamophobia in America*

"At a time when negative stereotypes dominate the public perception of Islam and Muslims, our young people are sorely in need of positive role models who embody the highest ideals of what it means to live a life of dignity and purpose. Marston has filled that void with this gripping narrative of the life of Emir Abd el-Kader, a towering figure who inspires us all to a greater sense of humanity and justice no matter what religion we may practice."

—**Robert F. Shedinger**, Luther College, author of *Was Jesus a Muslim?*

"Abd el-Kader—a man of principle, Muslim spiritual leader, diplomat, Arab luminary—led a rich and engaged life, despite decades of exile. This Algerian hero's story provides a fascinating window into the history of the nineteenth century, reflecting social and religious values and the tumultuous political times, and helping us make connections between France's brutal colonial policies, the Algerians' valiant resistance, and one leader's dignified and powerful struggle for justice. Marston's is an important contribution to youth literature, and will doubtless be a truly lasting one."

—**Zeina Azzam**, Georgetown University, Director of Educational Outreach, Center for Contemporary Arab Studies

D0206917

"The special merit of Marston's very beautiful book is that the virtues and human qualities of Abd el-Kader play a central role in her story. In bringing this story to American youth, the author is offering them the chance to discover not only the values of mercy and peace within Islam, but also the life of a person who completely embodied those values. This book is not only a beautiful narrative that is based on solid documentation, but it is above all a useful book for our children who are going to inherit a world which is in urgent need of mercy and peace."

    —**Ahmed Bouyerdene**, author of *Emir Abd el-Kader: Hero and Saint of Islam*

"Award-winning author Elsa Marston's books about the Middle East are often categorized as 'juvenile fiction and non-fiction.' However, *The Compassionate Warrior*, like most of her work, is a piece of solid scholarship, engagingly narrated, that will also have great appeal for adults. The Emir Abd el-Kader is an inspirational figure from Algerian history who deserves to be better known, and this exceptional book is a welcome contribution to that cause."

    —**Laurence Michalak**, University of California, Berkeley

"Elsa Marston's biography illuminates the extraordinary story of Emir Abd el-Kader. This 19th century hero was tireless in his efforts to protect innocent lives and the honor of Islam. His example is an inspiration for us all."

    —**Jacqueline Jules,** librarian and teacher, author of *Sarah Laughs* and *Benjamin and the Silver Goblet*

"*The Compassionate Warrior* provides us with a rich opportunity to learn about the life and teachings of a prominent Muslim spiritual teacher who resisted French colonialism. Not being content with returning violence for violence, Emir Abd el-Kader also protected Syrian Christians at a later point in his life. . . . This volume is highly recommended for all who seek to learn about spiritual ways of responding to the traumas of the contemporary world."

    —**Omid Safi**, University of North Carolina at Chapel Hill, author of *Memories of Muhammad: Why the Prophet Matters*

"In her engaging biography, the author shows well how Emir Abd el-Kader, head of a religious order and a fighter against colonial intrusions, preached tolerance and coexistence among communities, as was evident of his defense of the downtrodden during the exceptional Damascus riots of 1860. It is good of the author to bring to light the tolerance of a brave and compassionate hero who was needed then and is needed now as a model of leadership."

—**Leila Fawaz**, Tufts University, author of *An Occasion for War: Mount Lebanon and Damascus in 1860*

"In Elsa Marston's story of Emir Abd el-Kader we learn about the character of a man who was regularly faced with difficult decisions. In his journey, we see that being a warrior does not always mean going to war, but can also involve simply fighting for what is right. We witness the heroism that lies in human nature, even during the horror of battle, and the compassion that makes heroism possible. There is no avoiding the strong sense of justice that permeates all of his actions, and that that commitment to justice is deeply informed by his faith and spirituality. The remarkable nature of his story only highlights the importance of being true to one's convictions. His story is both awe-inspiring and inspirational."

—**Hussein Rashid**, Hofstra University, associate editor of *Religion Dispatches magazine*

"It is not very often that we readers and teachers come across a book that reveals so much history and biography in such an engaging and compelling way. Although the life of the great Algerian freedom fighter of the nineteenth century is the central focus of the book, the story also features French and North African colonial history, Christian-Muslim relations, and European politics. This book is an excellent vehicle for young people to explore a fast-moving story of heroic resistance to power, of nobility in times of war, of famous people and trying times, while all along learning—and probably enjoying—history, ethics, cross-cultural relations, and the inner workings of Muslim societies."

—**Roger Gaetani**, editor of *Introduction to Sufism: The Inner Path of Islam* and *A Spirit of Tolerance: The Inspiring Life of Tierno Bokar*, former teacher and developer of educational materials

ABOUT THE EMIR ABD EL-KADER

"The most redoubtable adversary that France encountered on African soil, the man who for sixteen years of heroic battles fought for his faith and for the independence of his country, Abd el-Kader is, unquestionably, the most important personage that has arisen in the last century among the Muslim populations."
   —*Le Figaro*, French national newspaper

"There are few names in the list of modern notabilities which are better known than that of the 'Arab Napoleon,' the warrior who, in defense of his native soil, successfully defied, during several campaigns, the whole power of France, and kept her armies in a state of almost unremitting warfare for more than fifteen years. . . . [The Emir Abd el-Kader] was one of the few great men of the century."
   —*The New York Times*

"Abd el-Kader disquieted Paris and challenged all the might of France in the reign of Louis Phillipe. The history of the French conquest of Algeria is in substance the record of the conflict which Abd el-Kader waged almost single-handed against the foremost military nation of Europe."
   —*The London Times*

"Emir Abd el-Kader was one of the most remarkable figures in recent Islamic history, combining perfection in both the active and the contemplative life, an achievement that remains of great significance today for Muslims and non-Muslims alike."
   —**Seyyed Hossein Nasr**, The George Washington University, author of *The Heart of Islam: Enduring Values for Humanity*

". . . the unsung hero of Algerian nationalism, Emir Abd el-Kader was a compassionate warrior and negotiator with the French, as well as a defender of religious minorities in the Ottoman Empire."
   —**Imam Feisal Abdul Rauf**, author of *What's Right with Islam* and *Moving the Mountain*

"Abd el-Kader acted towards me with a greatness that I would not have encountered in the most civilized countries of Europe."

—**de Marandol**, French prisoner-of-war in Algeria

"[The Emir Abd el-Kader] continues to be regarded in our times as the Muslim hero par excellence—a hero in whom the most noble chivalry was combined with the metaphysical insights of a true sage, and the spiritual graces of a realized saint."

—**Reza Shah-Kazemi**, Institute of Ismaili Studies, author of *My Mercy Encompasses All* and *The Other in the Light of the One*

"Today the Christian world unites to honor in the dethroned Prince of Islam [Abd el-Kader], the most unselfish of knightly warriors, risking limb and life to rescue his ancient foes, his conquerors and the conquerors of his race and his religion, from outrage and from death."

—*The New York Times*, October 20, 1860, reporting on the Emir's rescue of over 10,000 Christians in Damascus, Syria

"Abd el-Kader's most renowned deed was the rescue, at great risk to his own life, of over 10,000 Christians who were under all-out onslaught from an army of Druze in Damascus in 1860, an act which attracted the warm acclaim of such figures as Abraham Lincoln, Pope Pius IX, and Napoleon III."

—**William Stoddart**, author of *What Does Islam Mean in Today's World?*

"Such is the history of the man for whom our town is named. A scholar, a philosopher, a lover of liberty; a champion of his religion, a born leader of men, a great soldier, a capable administrator, a persuasive orator, a chivalrous opponent; the selection was well made, and with those pioneers of seventy years ago, we do honor the Shaykh."

—**Elkader High School**, Elkader, Iowa, class of 1915

THE
COMPASSIONATE WARRIOR
ABD EL-KADER OF ALGERIA

THE COMPASSIONATE WARRIOR

ABD EL-KADER OF ALGERIA

BY

ELSA MARSTON

FOREWORD BY
BARBARA PETZEN

✦Wisdom Tales✦

The Compassionate Warrior: Abd el-Kader of Algeria
© 2013 Wisdom Tales

Wisdom Tales is an imprint of World Wisdom, Inc.

Lexile® measure—1160L
www.Lexile.com

Library of Congress Cataloging-in-Publication Data

Marston, Elsa.
 The compassionate warrior : Abd el-Kader of Algeria / by Elsa
Marston ; foreword by Barbara Petzen.
   pages cm
 Includes bibliographical references and index.
 ISBN 978-1-937786-10-6 (pbk. : alk. paper) 1. 'Abd al-Qadir ibn
Muhyi al-Din, Amir of Mascara, 1807?-1883. 2. Statesmen--Algeria--
Biography--Juvenile literature. 3. Soldiers--Algeria--Biography--Juvenile
literature. 4. Algeria--Kings and rulers--Biography--Juvenile literature.
I. Petzen, Barbara. II. Title.
 DT294.7.A3M37 2013
 965'.03092--dc23
 [B]
                                                         2013010124
 Printed on acid-free paper in the United States of America

For information address Wisdom Tales,
P.O. Box 2682, Bloomington, Indiana 47402-2682
www.wisdomtalespress.com

CONTENTS

Abd el-Kader, photo by Étienne Carjat, 1865

LIST OF ILLUSTRATIONS

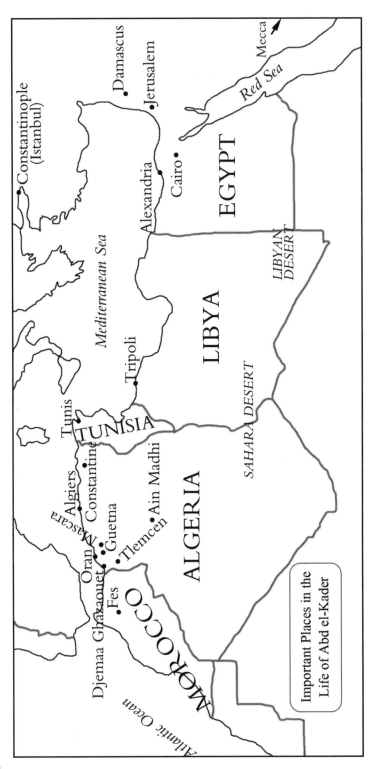

Important Places in the Life of Abd el-Kader

FOREWORD

ABD EL-KADER: WHAT MAKES A HERO?

When you ask most Americans to name a Muslim hero, you're likely to get blank stares . . . and perhaps eventually the name of a famous boxer or basketball player. Our media diet doesn't offer up many Muslims as role models—not because they don't exist, but because a lack of knowledge and understanding helps to create current stereotypes of Muslims as fanatical or violent.

This book introduces us to a true Muslim hero, a man who combined the best qualities of a freedom fighter and a peacemaker. Often called the George Washington of Algeria, the Emir Abd el-Kader led his people in a long fight to resist the French conquest and colonization of their country. Although he did not achieve liberty for Algeria, Abd el-Kader stands in the company of other great modern-day heroes who championed the rights of their people—Mahatma Gandhi, Nelson Mandela, Martin Luther King, and many others. He led his people in war, but fought also to maintain his humanity and mercy through this long time of strife. His principles of honorable and merciful conduct in war precede the Geneva Conventions by a century.

THE COMPASSIONATE WARRIOR

But it is not just as a noble warrior that Abd el-Kader won global fame and respect. Through a life of imprisonment and exile, this Sufi scholar, who led his followers on Islam's spiritual path, met and impressed many of the leading figures of his day. He never wavered from his insistence that those of different faiths could not only coexist in peace, but should learn from one another. He believed that the truest expression of Islam is a life lived in brotherhood and generosity of spirit.

Abd el-Kader was a man of contrasting qualities. He was a scholar and a soldier, both principled and pragmatic. He was devoutly faithful and remarkably open-minded, raised with a traditional education and yet interested in many of the most modern ideas and technologies of his day. He exemplifies the inspirational qualities of great leaders everywhere—courage, empathy, charisma, determination—bringing them together in a framework of Islamic piety and contemporary knowledge. Elsa Marston's excellent biography presents his legacy as a model for young Muslims today searching for a way to be both true to their religious heritage and open to the best of the modern world, and for non-Muslims who are not exposed to enough Muslim voices of reason and compassion.

Barbara Petzen
Director, Middle East Connections

PREFACE

Abd el-Kader first came into my life in the late 1950s, when I was doing research on French education in colonial Algeria. The Algerian war for independence was in full swing, and I'd been asked to write a report to back up an international student group's support for the university students of Algeria—meaning primarily the Muslim Algerians. My project gave me the sense that I was contributing something, however small, to history.

As I hunkered down in Harvard University's library, reading everything I could find about the French in Algeria, naturally I came across references to Abd el-Kader. Just the highlights, though: young, dashing, and handsome, he led resistance to the French conquest in the 1830s and '40s—and later, somehow, saved the lives of many Christians in Damascus.

A few months after finishing my report on education in Algeria, I found myself in Lebanon at the American University of Beirut. There I met the young man who would become my husband, Iliya Harik. His career as a professor of political science at Indiana University led to many sojourns in the Arab world, which inspired my own career as an author for young people, specializing in the Middle East.

But I never forgot the Emir Abd el-Kader—and when, in the fall of 2010, I was invited to write a biography of the Emir for young adults, I couldn't say no. The immediate inspiration was the recently created Abd el-Kader Education Project. Its headquarters are in Elkader, Iowa, a small town actually named in honor of Abd el-Kader in 1846—improbable, but absolutely true! (One of the founders had been reading the American and British press about the Emir's guerilla war against the French army, and he wanted to express his admiration for this colorful hero.)

The people of Elkader have always taken pride in this unusual aspect of their history, and in 2009 a group decided to start an essay contest for high school students. While the ultimate purpose is to encourage positive awareness of Islam and Muslim-Americans, the story of Abd el-Kader provides an appropriate focus because of his remarkable, many-sided character and concerns—especially interfaith bridge-building. A just-published biography of the Emir by John W. Kiser, titled *Commander of the Faithful: The Life and Times of Emir Abd el-Kader*, well researched and highly readable, launched the Abd el-Kader Education Project brilliantly. At the same time, the Project's directors could see the additional need for a shorter, less detailed biography for teenage readers.

Moreover, our multi-ethnic, multi-faith American society certainly needs more books for young people that convey a positive view of Islam. What better way than true stories of individuals whose faith was—or is—an essential background to their accomplishments? What more dramatic and inspiring example than Abd el-Kader?

Learning about the Emir and writing his story has been a fascinating project for me, and all the more because of a curious personal connection that I discovered in the course of my research. Back in September of 1958 I was traveling to Beirut on a freighter, and one of the ports where we stopped was a small town in western Algeria. Its French name was Nemours, but in the past it was called Djemaa Ghazaouet, "pirates' base"—yes, the very place where Abd el-Kader laid down his sword in 1847. At the time of my visit, a full 111 years later, the Algerians were once again embroiled in a struggle for freedom, with France and the *colons*, or settlers, still determined to keep Algeria French. Yet four years later, in 1962, the wheel of fortune would turn again and Algeria would be free.

Today, the struggle for freedom, justice, and acceptance of diverse faiths goes on in North Africa, the Middle East, and elsewhere, including our own country. I hope that in telling the story of Abd el-Kader, I can bring more attention to his message of peaceful, constructive, and inclusive coexistence.

PROLOGUE: ALGERIA, DECEMBER 1847

Under a gray winter sky, the ship rolled in the storm-whipped waves. A journey by sea was an ordeal that Abd el-Kader had not encountered since his boyhood. It was unsettling, this motion over which he could have no control—so different from the feeling of oneness with his horse! He grieved as he watched the coastline of Algeria recede into the foggy distance, knowing that he would never see his beloved homeland again.

But why was he being sent to France? Surely, in a few days at most, the French generals could have found a ship that would take him to Egypt, as they had promised. Despite the long years of bitter warfare, Abd el-Kader trusted them to be men of honor.

Abd el-Kader had given *his* word of honor, after all. He had gone to the French officers in peace, to state that he would fight no longer. Fifteen years was long enough . . . fifteen years during which he had known the heights of power and the depths of adversity. By now his people and his land had suffered far too much for the struggle to continue.

He had made his terms clear. He would leave Algeria forever, asking in return only that his exile be in Egypt or another Arab country.

The French officers had agreed readily and had treated him with every courtesy. Enemies could not have made peace in a more respectful manner.

But now questions were growing in Abd el-Kader's mind.

After two gloomy days at sea, the small ship reached the port of Toulon on the southern coast of France. Necessary arrangements would have to be made in the countries to which Abd el-Kader might be exiled; that was understandable. To his surprise, however, he and his people were taken to a quarantine station—and then to a prison-like military fort. Abd el-Kader was aware that soldiers were guarding him at all times.

Days became weeks in the cold, grim fort. Abd el-Kader could get only vague replies to his repeated questions. The translator assigned to him, Daumas, was sympathetic, but decisions about Abd el-Kader's future were not in his hands. At one point Daumas suggested writing directly to the King of France, and Abd el-Kader promptly did so, with firmness and tact.

A few days later a secret message came back. Yes, the promise *would* be kept!

But the last day of February, 1848, two full months after Abd el-Kader had voluntarily laid down his sword, brought dismaying news. The king had suddenly given up his throne and fled from France. A completely new kind of government had taken over. Would it honor promises made by the former ruler?

Or had Abd el-Kader indeed been betrayed?

CHAPTER 1

BARBARY PIRATES AND
FRENCH ADVENTURES

The roots of the predicament in which Abd el-Kader found himself went deep in the entangled history of the two adversaries, France and Algeria. A look at this background will help set Abd el-Kader in his time and place—a dramatic setting for a man who became one of the most celebrated leaders of the nineteenth century.

ALGERIA, ON THE BARBARY COAST

In 1516 the port city of Algiers, situated in the region of North Africa now called Algeria, came under the rule of the Ottomans, a far-flung Muslim empire with its capital in Constantinople (now Istanbul, Turkey). The Ottoman sultan sent an elite corps of Turkish soldiers to take charge, and before long the whole territory was known as the Regency of Algiers. The Dey of Algiers, chosen by the top military men from among their number, was the supreme ruler of the country. Surrounded by intrigue and jealousy, however, deys usually did not last long in office.

As the Ottoman Empire grew weaker in the eighteenth century, the Regency became almost independent. But the ruling class was still Turkish, and they imposed heavy taxes on the indigenous people of Algeria while keeping order with a heavy hand. Occasionally some of the Algerian tribes rose up against the oppressive Turkish rule, but did not get far.

Meanwhile, Europeans had their own problems with the coast of North Africa. The Barbary states, as the regions around the main ports of Algiers, Tripoli (Libya), and Tunis (Tunisia) were known, were basically brigands. Lawlessness on the high seas was their main business—and a thriving business it was. The North African raiders, called corsairs, were not outlaws like pirates; quite the contrary, they worked for their governments. In their small, swift vessels they roamed the Mediterranean, preying on the ships of other states.

Of course they seized goods and treasure, but that was not the primary prize. What the corsairs wanted most were human beings. Some of the captives, brought back to the home base, were sold to private individuals, but most were thrown into large prisons and forced to work at heavy labor. They might languish as slaves for years, unless they were important or fortunate enough to be bought back by their governments or families. The Barbary states grew rich on ransom for unfortunate captives, most of them Christians from European countries.

Naturally, the Europeans feared and hated the Barbary corsairs. At the same time, European states had reasons for *not* putting an end to the business. Sometimes they were too occupied with their own wars to pay much attention to the corsairs in the Mediterranean, or they needed the Barbary states for alliances and food supplies. Consequently they made treaties with the rulers of Algiers, Tunis, and Tripoli, paying them tribute—large amounts of money, ridiculously extravagant gifts, and lots of firearms—to leave their ships alone.

Then a new player entered the field. The ships of the newly independent United States of America began getting captured in the Mediterranean, and the Americans were outraged. In 1803, ships from the United States Navy attacked Tripoli and put the corsairs of Tripoli out of business. (This expedition, which included a contingent of U.S. Marines, inspired a line in the Marines' Hymn: "From the halls of Montezuma to the shores of Tripoli.") The United States still had to pay tribute to Algiers and Tunis, however, so in 1815 the American navy took on the Barbary states again. This time the Turkish rulers decided not to put up any fight at all. Great Britain, not to be outdone by the upstart Americans, promptly sent a formidable fleet to attack Algiers in 1816. A massive ten-hour bombardment all but finished off the corsairs.

The Barbary states' long history left North Africa with a decidedly unsavory reputation. It was also quite a colorful one, inspiring many a best-selling memoir, novel, painting, opera, drama, poem, and ballet. A more realistic description, perhaps—and also important to keep in mind—came from the American consul in Algiers in the 1820s. Slavery was not as terrible as generally thought, he wrote, and the population was both pious and tolerant. Persons and property were safe day and night, the city prosperous, and the garbage collected regularly. Learning flourished, with many Islamic schools and other religious institutions.

Nonetheless, for three hundred years a small, alien ruling class, supported by brigandage, kidnapping, and extortion, had run much of North Africa. It had dominated a vastly larger indigenous population with no reason whatever for loyalty toward their rulers. This was the society that faced the French when they arrived at Algiers in 1830.

FRANCE ON THE EVE OF CONQUEST

For hundreds of years France had been one of the most prominent nation-states in Europe. The French regarded their culture as the finest possible, whether in literature, philosophy, architecture, science, or cuisine. At the time of its fateful encounter with Algeria, however, France was torn by political divisions.

In the late eighteenth century, the French people had overthrown their monarchy, their nobility, and the Catholic Church in one of the bloodiest and most passionately ideological revolutions in history. The French Revolution (1789-94) was followed by a republican form of government, which soon yielded to the ambitions of one man: Napoleon Bonaparte. Bonaparte set out with his armies to spread the ideals of the French republic—liberty, fraternity, equality—all over Europe, but the other European states wanted no part of it. In 1815, when a coalition led by Great Britain finally put down the French threat, the monarchs of Europe breathed much more easily. France, too, went back to being a monarchy.

The French were not very happy with their king, Charles X. Many looked back on Bonaparte's era as a time of great national glory. They mourned the loss of prestige from his final defeat, and they longed to see the French army redeem itself on the field of battle. Moreover, King Charles' government tried to undo many of the progressive changes that the Revolution had brought about, and the country's economy was in bad shape. The middle class—and public opinion—grew steadily more powerful.

By the mid-1820s France was bristling with nationalistic fervor and eager to flex its muscles. It soon found a way to do so, thanks to an incident that sounds almost like low comedy.

During the Napoleonic wars, the government of France had been forced to buy wheat from the Regency of Algiers and had run up a huge debt. *That* France, however, was the republican government. Now France was a monarchy again, and in no mood to pay debts incurred by irresponsible revolutionaries. One day in April 1827, the French consul made this very clear to the ruler of Algiers. Finally losing patience, the dey struck the Frenchman with his fly whisk.

In Paris the royalist government was outraged by this insult to French honor. It recalled the consul and set up a naval blockade. In Algiers, the dey ordered all French citizens to leave.

If a swat with peacock feathers had been the only issue, no doubt the matter could have been settled without bloodshed. But France was ready for dramatic action, and the unpopular government of King Charles X wanted to divert attention from its troubles at home. Although some people argued fiercely against military action, calling it a shameless, self-deluded adventure, the nation went ahead anyway and prepared for war. On June 14, 1830, France launched an assault against the city of Algiers.

THE FRENCH CONQUEST OF 1830

This was no small punitive raid. The French fleet—one hundred warships and five hundred and seventy-two supply vessels—carried the freshly created Army of Africa consisting of thirty-one thousand soldiers, five hundred cavalrymen, and more than a thousand engineers. The expedition also included cannons, four thousand horses, and several artists—the photo-journalists of the time.

In the face of overwhelming firepower, Algiers fell quickly. The dey and his family speedily departed for Egypt, leaving behind a fabulous treasury of gold and jewels. The Turkish military and the whole ruling class likewise fled or were soon expelled, leaving behind a capital city without anyone who could manage anything.

Soon after declaring victory, the triumphant French general made a public announcement promising to protect houses of worship and to respect the inhabitants' rights. Those words were quickly forgotten, and the French soldiers fell to looting and destroying Algiers. They desecrated mosques, ripped houses apart for firewood, used manuscripts from libraries for their bivouac fires, and massacred many of the people. Everywhere the French invaders went in the central part of Algeria, they destroyed. The urban populations all but vanished, taking flight to the countryside or dying of starvation or disease. French observers, including some sent by Parliament in 1833 to report on conditions, were horrified.

Although the French had easily conquered Algiers with their impressive military force, they had no clear idea of what to do next. They had made no plans for a new system of government, and they knew practically nothing about Algeria and its people.

Then, with chaos reigning in Algiers, the French king suddenly quit his office and fled from Paris. Another royal head took on the crown in late July, Louis-Philippe, promising better government. But France was torn between royalists and republicans, and could not agree about Algeria. The French generals, government, and public argued over their choices. Should they limit their North African possessions to the main coastal cities, such as Algiers, Oran, Bone? Or should they try to conquer the entire country? Or should they just wash their hands of the whole undertaking and go home?

Very soon the third option was no longer possible. Barely had most of the people of Algiers been cleared out than European settlers started arriving, seeing it as a chance for a better life. Some people in France thought Algeria would be a good place to dump society's riffraff—the poor, criminal, and politically troublesome. In any case, settlers rapidly established facts on the ground, seizing land everywhere they could and dispossessing the Algerians.

CHAPTER 1: BARBARY PIRATES & FRENCH ADVENTURES

It is hard to understand why, at the very beginning of the conflict—even before the French themselves had suffered losses, horrors, and humiliations—they should have behaved so brutally. Possibly it was revenge for those centuries of Barbary piracy and the enslavement of Christians . . . possibly it was racial and religious prejudice. In any case, the conquest of Algiers was a forewarning of what lay ahead for the two peoples. Not only would the North African Muslims be conquered by military force, but their property, culture, and lives would be deliberately destroyed—all in the name of European superiority.

Yet from the start there were other, more idealistic, motives present in the French adventure. However hypocritical and dishonest they may now appear, these expressions of a noble purpose should not be overlooked, for they carried some weight throughout the history of France in Algeria. The idea of France's "civilizing mission," as it was called, soon found its way into speeches and memoirs. For instance, in 1832 a high-ranking French administrator wrote:

> To pacify and enlighten these countries by turn, and extend
> again the benefits of science that have been lost for so many
> centuries: that is the noble mission which she [France] has
> proposed for herself and which she will accomplish.[1]

The two opposing drives—conquest versus civilization—pulled and ripped at the French presence in Algeria from the very first days till the last, with aftershocks still felt today. Certainly Abd el-Kader experienced this "split personality" of France in North Africa. It's at the center of his dramatic story.

CHAPTER 2

AN UNLIKELY LEADER EMERGES

When the French invaded Algiers, they assumed that their main task was simply to get rid of the Turkish overlords, and then somehow everything would fall into place. For a few more years, the Ottomans held cities in other parts of the Regency, but for the most part the Turks gave up quickly. Their departure left a dangerous power vacuum. At last the French had to face the native population of Algeria—and for this challenge they were totally unprepared.

THE ALGERIANS

Who were the Algerians? The people of Algeria, who totaled about three million (a very rough estimate), were almost entirely Muslim but of two main ethnic backgrounds. The Arabs, the majority, were descended from Arab conquerors who brought Islam to North Africa in the eighth century C.E. The Berbers, also called Kabyles, were the original inhabitants of the land, from ancient times. They had adopted Islam and to some extent the Arabic language, but most lived in the rugged Kabyle mountains, apart from the rest of the population. A few thousand Jews, active in trade and finance, lived in the main cities.

There were very few, if any, native Christians.

Outside the cities—only five to ten percent of the total population—Algeria was a traditional tribal society. A vast land, a little larger than the entire United States east of the Mississippi River, it was home to many different tribes, large and small. Some tribes, settled in the fertile plains, made their living in agriculture. Others, in the arid and rugged mountainous areas, were nomadic, roaming over the land with their flocks of sheep and goats.

There were two main political groupings of tribes. One was called the *makhzen* tribes, with warrior skills, values, and traditions. They had served the Turkish overlords in collecting taxes and keeping the peace, and naturally they wanted to hold onto their power and privileges. The other, called the *rayah* tribes ("the flock"), were settled and peaceful; they were dominated by the *makhzen* tribes.

From the *rayah* tribes came the marabouts, men—and very rarely, women—of exceptional devoutness and wisdom. Often well educated and believed to have a divine blessing called *baraka*, the marabouts were the religious and intellectual aristocracy. Although the status of marabout was hereditary, an individual marabout still had to earn respect by demonstrating good character and high standards of conduct and piety. The warlike *makhzen* tribes looked down on the *rayah* tribes and especially disliked the marabouts. The Turkish overlords kept the tribes weak by playing them off against each other.

REACTION TO THE FRENCH INVASION

At first the tribes had no idea what to expect of the French invasion. Would the French be like the Spaniards, who had held parts of the coast in past centuries without causing too much trouble? No, as the Algerians soon learned, this European intrusion would be very different.

THE COMPASSIONATE WARRIOR

With the Ottoman rulers gone and no new system of law and order in place, the country fell into anarchy. The tribes, valuing their independence and competitive strength more than cooperation, seized the chance to fight, raid, and settle old scores—which naturally weakened them further. The Algerians were not, however, completely overwhelmed at the start. With Europeans already moving into Algiers and starting to change street names, some of the tribes in that area put aside their rivalries and worked together to harass the French. For two or three years they prevented the invaders from occupying several important towns.

In the western part of the country, where the story of Abd el-Kader starts, the tribes were less affected by the French invasion. Many, in fact, were indifferent to the threat, so long as they could continue in their independent ways. When the French seized the major port of Oran, however, and the system of control by *makhzen* tribes broke down, lawlessness took over.

In the midst of this disorder, there was one man, an esteemed marabout, who could command obedience. Muhyi ad-Din, the father of Abd el-Kader, claimed descent from the prophet Muhammad, a source of great prestige, and belonged to one of the most powerful tribes in the area. He was also the leader of a religious brotherhood called the Qadiriyya, which had started in Baghdad centuries earlier. These brotherhoods, widespread in the Muslim world, practiced a form of Islam called Sufism, which encouraged belief in direct communion with God through mysticism and prayer. In North Africa the center of the Qadiriyya brotherhood was in a village called Guetna, near the important town of Mascara in the region of Oran. Although Guetna was a small place, the Qadiriyya brotherhood became famous for its school and other religious activities.

The Turks had long regarded the marabouts as subversive and tried to suppress them. Now, with the Turks gone and the country gripped by anarchy, the marabouts became natural leaders. Muhyi ad-Din not only had stature among the tribes but was respected by the Sultan of Morocco, just to the west of Algeria. The sultan appointed Muhyi ad-Din as his *khalifa*, meaning "lieutenant" or deputy. This gave Muhyi ad-Din, who had always resented the Ottoman overlords, a means of taking action against them. Leading other tribal chiefs and their men, he set out to drive the last of the Turks from western Algeria.

By this time, 1832, the French had teamed up with the remaining Turkish forces and powerful *makhzen* tribes—odd allies indeed—and had established garrisons in Oran and a few other towns on the coast. As a result the French, along with the Turks, became Muhyi ad-Din's target. Between April and November of 1832 he led many attacks on the French garrison in Oran, but with no success.

It was definitely not wasted effort, however. Muhyi ad-Din's son Abd el-Kader, about twenty-four years of age, came into his own during these skirmishes. Brave in battle and skillful as a leader, he even seemed to have a charmed life. In spite of the risks he took—sometimes mocking the French cannon balls as they whizzed past—he was never wounded. This added to popular beliefs that he had special powers and divine protection.

Both Muhyi ad-Din and Abd el-Kader, it must be remembered, were marabouts, men of religion and learning. They had no training in warfare, and no fondness for fighting. But when it appeared to be necessary, they did not hesitate to throw themselves into battle. And they were astonishingly good at it.

ABD EL-KADER'S EARLY YEARS

Abd el-Kader was born in 1807 (or 1808, according to some sources) in the village of Guetna. He was not the first-born of Muhyi ad-Din's sons—he had at least two older brothers. But from his birth, his father had sensed that he was a highly gifted child and had given him special attention. The son and grandson of important marabouts, Abd el-Kader was conscious of living up to his heritage from an early age. His mother, Lalla Zohra, also had great influence on him. A person of good sense and ability, she was also literate and well educated about religion, which was most unusual for a woman at that time. She played a strong supporting role throughout Abd el-Kader's life.

Growing up in Guetna gave Abd el-Kader rare advantages from the start. He received an excellent education at the Qadiriyya brotherhood's *zawiya*, which his father directed. A *zawiya*, something like a European monastery, was a center for learning, religious instruction, and prayer. It also served as a hostel for the many students who came from far distances for higher studies there—and a refuge for people fleeing the painful grip of Ottoman justice.

The young Abd el-Kader seems to have excelled at just about everything he undertook. At the *zawiya* he studied Arabic grammar, Islamic law, and the holy book of Islam called the Koran. In addition he spent time with a scholar in another village learning mathematics, Greek philosophy, astronomy and geography, history, veterinary science, and even plant pharmacology. When he was fourteen, his father sent him to a school in Oran for further study. His year in town made Abd el-Kader aware of the lure of luxury and worldly pleasures—but they were not for him. Shocked by the arrogant and loose behavior of the Turks, Abd el-Kader focused all the more on what he regarded as the basic, true values of Islam. He was very glad to come home to the simple life at Guetna.

A strikingly handsome man, with dark blue eyes and a high forehead, Abd el-Kader stood a little on the short side but was extremely fit and strong. Even as a child he was known for his horsemanship. As an adult he could manage a horse under all conditions, including desert survival, and could endure extraordinarily long hours in the saddle, covering great distances. This physical strength and stamina would serve him well in the years to come.

At the age of fifteen Abd el-Kader was married to his cousin, Kheira, as was customary for a youth in his social position. It proved a good marriage, although she probably saw very little of him for many years. Over time, Abd el-Kader had additional wives, since Islam permits a man to marry up to four women; but Kheira, mother of three of his children, was always his favorite and a trusted advisor.

In the fall of 1824, Muhyi ad-Din decided—over his wife's objections—to take Abd el-Kader on pilgrimage to the holy cities in Arabia, an important religious duty expected of every Muslim if at all possible. Many members of their tribe accompanied them. The religious purpose was undoubtedly of paramount importance, but there may also have been a political motive behind Muhyi ad-Din's decision to depart at this time. He knew he was suspected of stirring up the tribes against the Ottoman rulers, and the only way he could escape arrest—without appearance of guilt—was to go on pilgrimage. In any case, his plans soon went awry.

The Ottoman ruler of Oran, Bey Hasan, had imprisoned Muhyi ad-Din in the past. Now, learning about the large caravan of pilgrims headed eastward, he grew suspicious. He had Muhyi ad-Din and Abd el-Kader arrested, and they had good reason to fear for their lives. Fortunately the bey did not dare go that far; he kept them under house arrest in Oran for about a year before finally allowing them to continue on their travels.

Muhyi ad-Din and Abd el-Kader reached the holy city of Mecca for the pilgrimage and then traveled far and wide over the Middle East. They spent time in Alexandria, Cairo, Damascus, Baghdad, and even the Christian monastery of Saint Catherine in the heart of the Sinai Peninsula. Abd el-Kader took advantage of the famous mosques and Islamic universities on his itinerary, pursuing his deep interest in religion and philosophy. Baghdad was a particularly important stop because it was the burial place of the medieval Sufi mystic who had founded the Qadiriyya brotherhood to which Muhyi ad-Din and Abd el-Kader belonged. Abd al-Qadir al-Jilani had lived in the twelfth century C.E. when Baghdad was a great center of learning, and preached acceptance of the value of all religions. Muhyi ad-Din and Abd el-Kader regarded him as a greatly esteemed ancestor.

Toward the end of 1827 the father and son returned home, "their resources used up, their bodies aching, but their souls full."[1] On their arrival in Guetna they were showered with honor and affection, and the celebrations lasted for weeks. Afraid that all the excitement might make the suspicious Bey Hasan come after them again, Muhyi ad-Din decided to keep out of the public eye for a year or so. He and Abd el-Kader therefore devoted themselves to study and prayer, in this way avoiding the bey's prisons while gaining in prestige among the tribes for their reputation of piety.

ABD EL-KADER STEPS FORWARD

This brings the story up to the first years of the French conquest and Muhyi ad-Din's efforts to restore some kind of order in western Algeria. He had more in mind.

In November 1832, the Algerians finally took a rest after failing to dislodge the French from Oran. The tribal chiefs convened and argued for an organized, sustained campaign. Muhyi ad-Din, explaining that he was no longer physically able to continue the fight, proposed that his son take over for him. Earlier, when he had suggested this, the other chiefs had refused; but now, after Abd el-Kader's good showing in battle, they willingly accepted him as their leader.

How did Abd el-Kader respond? His natural inclinations were for quiet, peaceful pursuits—but he was also a most obedient and loyal son. He, too, readily accepted this sudden and drastic change in his life.

In the most important mosque in the nearby town of Mascara, before a large assembly including tribal chiefs, marabouts, and leaders of the Jewish community, a formal ceremony gave Abd el-Kader the title "emir" (commander, prince) and designated him "Commander of the Faithful." He was twenty-five years old. In any military campaign it would have been remarkable for a man so young to take command . . . all the more so in a society where age and experience were as esteemed as in the traditional Muslim world.

Abd el-Kader clearly had the natural qualities for the job, and his family's status and background added to his prestige. Something else, besides the widespread common longing for a good leader, also worked in his favor: the hold of mystical religious beliefs among his people. For years, in fact, miraculous stories about his birth had been popular with the tribespeople. Now the story spread that while in Baghdad on the pilgrimage trip, Abd el-Kader and his father had met an old man who referred to a "sultan"—supreme ruler—in their group. Yes, people said, the old man must actually have been the famous medieval saint Abd al-Qadir al-Jilani himself, and he was referring to the young Abd el-Kader as a future ruler.

Muhyi ad-Din made a point of publicizing these stories, speaking often of mysterious dream-like encounters in which greatness was predicted for Abd el-Kader. Very possibly he had been hoping—long before the French appeared on the scene—that someday Abd el-Kader would lead popular resistance to the Turkish oppression. The "miracle" stories circulated among the tribes like a finishing touch to Muhyi ad-Din's plans for his son.

The drama was ready for its hero, and Abd el-Kader was perfectly cast in the role.

CHAPTER 3

THE EMIR'S STRATEGY

With the backing of three of the most important western tribes, Abd el-Kader was now the leader of resistance to the French invaders in that area. What sort of a commander would he be? Would this quiet marabout really have the skills and courage needed to carry on prolonged and fierce warfare?

A couple of years earlier, Abd el-Kader had given a strong demonstration of his political wisdom and his powers of persuasion. As the Ottoman system was falling apart in the months following the French invasion, Bey Hasan—the same man who had imprisoned Muhyi ad-Din and Abd el-Kader on their pilgrimage trip—appealed to Muhyi ad-Din for protection. Strange twist of fate! Muhyi ad-Din called a family council, who decided that honor demanded generosity. But Abd el-Kader, only twenty-three at that time, pointed out that if something should happen to their "guest" while under their protection—as indeed it might, given his well-known lack of popularity—Muhyi ad-Din would be held responsible and the prestige of his family would suffer. Abd el-Kader's views, expressed with the gift of eloquence that served him all his life, convinced the others. Bey Hasan was advised to look elsewhere.

THE COMPASSIONATE WARRIOR

THE EMIR TAKES CHARGE

Abd el-Kader had little time, however, in which to demonstrate his ability to deal with hard realities. He was well aware that he would have to manage the envy, ambition, and hostility running throughout tribal society. The *makhzen* tribes, afraid of losing their entrenched privileges, especially resented the new Emir.

His most pressing job, therefore, was to restore law and order, which meant winning over the tribes and chiefs who had not yet declared their support. Many were scornful of his youth. Most, determined to keep their own power, would prove disloyal unless thoroughly convinced of his strong leadership. Abd el-Kader could use persuasion with those who would listen, but he would have to undermine, outwit, or overpower those who refused. He went about the job of consolidating his strength in a manner that was well planned, deliberate, and when necessary, ruthless.

Sending messages to all the tribes in the western district, Abd el-Kader made three points clear. First, he, the Emir Abd el-Kader, had been elected as the authentic leader of the western tribes. Second, his leadership would accord strictly with Islamic law and principles, and he would expect the same of his followers' behavior. Third—and perhaps most important in the eyes of the tribesmen—he would lead *jihad* against the European invaders. As his father had found earlier, it would be next to impossible to motivate the tribes unless they were convinced that they were fighting a *jihad*.

What did *jihad* mean to Abd el-Kader? The basic meaning of this often puzzling concept is "struggle." For most Muslims this usually means individual moral struggle—against temptation, bad thoughts, and wicked acts: anything that would weaken a person's being a good Muslim. But *jihad* also has an "outward" expression, leading to actual combat. In such cases, the struggle should be for a religious purpose, typically described as "defending Islam and Muslims."

For the Algerians under Abd el-Kader, *jihad* was indeed a "holy war." This did not mean converting the Christian invaders to Islam, nor harming Christian Europe. Rather, *jihad* meant the defense of Muslim people against the attack of non-Muslim outsiders. If necessary, defense could even mean *offense*: waging offensive campaigns against the threatening forces.

But what would be the ultimate objective of Abd el-Kader's *jihad*? That was not so clear. To drive every last European from the shores of Algeria would be neither reasonable nor necessary. In any case, Abd el-Kader knew that if he wanted the tribes to follow him, he would have to call loudly and unmistakably for *jihad*—even though *jihad* might sometimes be more of a strategy than an absolute demand.

In addition to motivation, the Emir needed a capital city that would demonstrate his supremacy. The village of his birth, Guetna, was too small, so he chose the nearby town of Mascara, which had a strategic location and many centuries of history and culture. His triumphal entry to Mascara, in November 1832, helped win the allegiance of more tribes. As everyone could see, here was a man who, in spite of his youth, could indeed command!

Another of the Emir's useful assets was his Sufi brotherhood, the Qadiriyya. The various brotherhoods tended to compete with each other, so Abd el-Kader actively promoted his own. He sent out agents to promote the Qadiriyya beliefs and help establish new centers in both towns and tribal areas. This strategy helped widen and consolidate his control, while encouraging more support for his cause.

Meanwhile, there was a challenge to Abd el-Kader's power from the Sultan of Morocco, Abd ar-Rahman, to whom many of the western

THE COMPASSIONATE WARRIOR

Algerian tribes were loyal. Abd el-Kader found ways to turn the sultan's strength to his own advantage. He widely promoted the idea that he, too, was subject to Abd ar-Rahman's authority and that he was, in fact, governing in the sultan's name. He even publicized a document, said to be a letter from Abd ar-Rahman, that expressed support for the Emir. In short, he used every stratagem and ploy he could to consolidate his forces.

All this time, Muhyi ad-Din was working vigorously as his son's agent, traveling from tribe to tribe, explaining the importance of what Abd el-Kader was doing and winning their support. But on July 20, 1833, Muhyi ad-Din died suddenly. Even this grievous loss worked to Abd el-Kader's advantage, however, because it seemed to fulfill a prophecy from one of Muhyi ad-Din's dreams about Abd el-Kader becoming the new leader. This helped convince people that Muhyi ad-Din's *baraka*, the blessing believed to have been divinely bestowed on him, would now rest on Abd el-Kader.

CONFRONTING THE FRENCH

Having managed to win the allegiance of most of the tribes in the western province, this marabout-warrior now felt ready to take on the French army in Oran. With their far superior training and weaponry, the French forces could have defeated the Algerians fairly easily. In spite of this, they did not have the manpower both to fight in the countryside and to hold on to the territory they had won. Moreover, the European style of warfare, with its pitched battles, would not work in dealing with the Arabs' irregular method of fighting. Therefore the French chose to stay inside the walls of Oran, occasionally going out to make punitive raids on villages.

With his adversaries more or less locked up, Abd el-Kader could pursue his own strategy. Experience had shown him that direct military assaults on Oran would only sacrifice more fighting men. The essential move, he decided, was a siege of the French enclaves on the coast, the enemy-held towns of Oran, Mostaghanem, and Arzew. He would have to disrupt the trade in livestock, grain, and produce that certain tribes were engaging in with the French enemy. This trade, at inflated prices, had produced much wealth for some Algerians, and naturally they did not want to lose it. Earlier, when Muhyi ad-Din was still the leader of the cooperating tribes, he had faced the same problem and had dealt with it harshly. Anyone caught supplying the French with provisions suffered the loss of his ears, nose, and one hand.

Abd el-Kader took an even more drastic step, declaring that anyone who defied his orders against trading with the French would be executed. These measures, showing that he meant business, helped him successfully impose a siege on the three French-held towns. The invaders were forced to depend on food and provisions supplied by sea from France, which was both hazardous and costly.

Meanwhile the French had been inflicting considerable damage. The general in charge of Oran ordered such ruthless massacres of villagers that he became notorious for his cruelty. In April 1833, however, a shift in command put the conflict on quite a different footing. A new general, Louis-Alexis Desmichels, took charge of Oran and soon became painfully aware of the hardships caused by Abd el-Kader's siege. He could also see that his occasional forays against the tribes were only strengthening support for his adversary. He sent Abd el-Kader a proposal for an exchange of prisoners—and a peace treaty.

A DOUBLE-EDGED TREATY WITH THE ENEMY

In his response to this opening, Abd el-Kader demonstrated his grasp of political strategy. He rejected Desmichels' letter almost rudely. Then, a little later he instructed his agent in Oran, an Algerian Jew skilled at dealing with both Europeans and Arabs, to suggest that the general try again. Desmichels did so. This time Abd el-Kader pointed out that according to Islamic law, peace *could* be considered—provided the offer came first from the non-Muslim side. To Desmichels' third letter, Abd el-Kader responded courteously. In February 1834, through translators and other intermediaries, a treaty was worked out to the satisfaction of both sides.

But not to *everyone's* satisfaction. This curious agreement, usually known as the Desmichels Treaty, was actually *two* treaties, one in French and the other in Arabic. In certain important respects they were actually contradictory—yet both were considered legally valid. The Arabic version contained a secret clause recognizing Abd el-Kader as the controlling power in the western half of Algeria. The government in Paris naturally expected just the opposite: they wanted France recognized as the superior power. By the time they learned the truth, the treaty was already signed and they could do nothing about it.

Under the Desmichels Treaty—the Arabic version—the French retained control over the ports of Oran, Mostaghanem, and Arzew. Subject to the Emir's permission, they could trade in the territory he controlled. The French prisoners (four soldiers who had been caught in an ambush) were released. In return, France would recognize the Emir's sovereignty over the rest of the western province, plus his monopoly on trade. The treaty was a diplomatic triumph for Abd el-Kader and brought a stop to hostilities and bloodshed—for a while.

Why did Abd el-Kader and General Desmichels both agree to a treaty that would, in some ways, seem to be the opposite of what they wanted? In Abd el-Kader's case, he had to give up the call for *jihad*, which had been so important in rallying the tribes to accept his leadership. He also had to allow the French army to hold the coastal towns, and even protect them if necessary. But apparently he considered this a fair price to pay for what he really wanted: breathing space. He needed time to consolidate his power, which now extended over more than half of Algeria, and to revive and organize his people. His objectives were growing more ambitious and complex.

As for Desmichels, he evidently thought it in the best interest of France to have a firm alliance with the strongest power among the Algerians. Indeed, he appears to have bent over backward to strengthen Abd el-Kader. He not only helped the Emir extend his authority eastward, he also generously supplied arms and military advice—as though Abd el-Kader was the partner of France rather than the adversary.

Not surprisingly, the peace achieved by the Desmichels Treaty was fragile. The fuzzy question of who was sovereign over whom angered the French, who were also upset about Abd el-Kader's monopoly of trade. Early in 1835 Desmichels was recalled—but apparently not in disgrace, as he went on to have a satisfactory military career.

The new commander at Oran, General Trézel, promptly tried to set matters straight—for France. In June of 1835, he sent a military expedition against Abd el-Kader. It was a disaster. Abd el-Kader's men ambushed and utterly destroyed the French forces in swampy stretches around the Macta River. Although the Algerians also lost many men, it was an important victory for them and a devastating blow to French morale.

For the French, the defeat at the Macta River demanded the severest possible retaliation. Abd el-Kader could see it coming, but his request to restore peace was refused by Count Bertrand Clauzel, one of the prominent generals during this period. He then set up a network of intelligence agents in the towns and also sought support from the British and American consuls, although without success.

THE COMPASSIONATE WARRIOR

As the Desmichels Treaty unraveled during the winter of 1835-36, Clauzel took his revenge. Several important towns, including the Emir's capital, Mascara, were destroyed. When a French officer entered Mascara after the bombardment, he reported:

> What I saw then was the most hideous spectacle I have ever witnessed. I had never imagined what a sacked city, where numerous inhabitants have been massacred, would be like. . . . Not a single object remained untouched, the houses were in flame. . .[1]

With insufficient manpower, the French again decided not to hold these ruined cities. Hence the countryside outside the French-held towns on the coast remained under Abd el-Kader's control.

RESISTANCE AND RIVALRY IN THE EASTERN PART OF ALGERIA

Although Abd el-Kader was now master of the larger part of Algeria and aiming to unify the entire country, another man was trying to do the same thing in the eastern part. Hajj Ahmed, from a powerful Algerian family in Constantine, had asserted himself as the new ruler of Constantine as soon as the Turks left. While he considered the area still part of the Ottoman Empire, he did make changes toward a fairer system of rule.

Inevitably a contest was shaping up between Hajj Ahmed and Abd el-Kader. In 1833 Hajj Ahmed asked the Ottoman sultan to designate him the ruler of the entire country. In 1835, after Abd el-Kader had called off the *jihad* because of the Desmichels Treaty, Ahmed tried to keep it going—in the Emir's territory.

The French tried repeatedly to win Hajj Ahmed's support, but he refused to recognize French control of any form. Finally, in the fall of

CHAPTER 3: THE EMIR'S STRATEGY

1836, General Clauzel decided to destroy Arab resistance in the eastern part of the country and sent an army of about seven thousand five hundred to seize Constantine. They met a thorough defeat.

This convinced the French Ministry of War that their armies could not fight simultaneously in different parts of the country. Since Abd el-Kader had shown willingness to negotiate, perhaps it was time to take him out of the picture again with another treaty? The French general who carried out these negotiations, Thomas-Robert Bugeaud, also wanted an interlude of peace. In May 1837 he signed a new agreement with Abd el-Kader, the Treaty of Tafna (a river in western Algeria), which ceded almost all of the western and central parts of Algeria to Abd el-Kader.

With the Emir observing peace for the time being, the French promptly set out to seek revenge for their humiliating defeat at Constantine a few months earlier. This time they succeeded, destroying a city that had been a center of learning and culture for hundreds of years. A large number of its inhabitants died, many of them falling into the gorges around the city while trying to flee. Hajj Ahmed escaped and remained a fugitive and guerilla fighter for several more years.

Abd el-Kader's decision to step out of the fight, when it was clear that the French were preparing for another assault on Constantine, raises questions. It could be seen as the Emir's way of getting back at Hajj Ahmed for his earlier challenges. There was more to the conflict than personal rivalry, however. The two men differed significantly in their views of Algeria's future. Hajj Ahmed wanted to continue Ottoman-style rule, based on traditional powerful families. Abd el-Kader, trying to revive a society weak for hundreds of years, wanted a much more progressive system. His vision for Algeria was, in fact, a truly revolutionary change from the past—and one of the most striking features of his fight for freedom.

CHAPTER 4

ABD EL-KADER'S VISION FOR HIS PEOPLE

Many a freedom fighter has led a brave struggle against oppression, but with little thought about what to do when the fighting was over. Abd el-Kader was different. He *did* know what he wanted for his people's future: a unified Algerian state with a government based on law and justice. But how does a leader create a new state, starting with almost nothing? Despite the ever-present threat of warfare on the horizon, Abd el-Kader's vision was so well planned and carried out that it deserves a close look.

WHAT ABD EL-KADER HAD TO WORK WITH

The Emir's new state would be almost completely different from the Ottoman regency. The old regime had depended on rulers from outside Algeria, with a social hierarchy that kept the native people at the bottom. Its practice of divide-and-rule was enforced by foreign soldiers, while a stagnant system of government permitted no political or social progress.

CHAPTER 4: ABD EL-KADER'S VISION FOR HIS PEOPLE

In contrast, Abd el-Kader wanted to put into action his devout commitment to Islam by building a society based on Islamic principles. No question of "separation of religion and state." To Abd el-Kader, and to most Muslims and many Christians at that time, good government was based on the proper understanding and practice of religion.

Thanks to the two treaties with the French, the Desmichels Treaty in 1834 and the Tafna Treaty of 1837, Abd el-Kader had about five years of peace—or rather, only intermittent warfare. This gave him the chance to try to make Algerian society more cohesive, lawful, and ultimately peaceful. It was not, however, just admirable principles that motivated the Emir. By being head of an organized political entity, he would have much more prestige and leverage than if he were simply the leader of a group of rebellious tribes. As a "worthy opponent," he could better resist the French adversaries during times of conflict, and bargain more successfully during the periods of peace.

In his efforts to consolidate tribal society, Abd el-Kader had to work within the existing system, knowing that he could not try to change it too quickly. But even moving carefully, he met resistance. Tribes would decide to break away whenever their confidence in him wavered, or when, for one reason or another, they felt it to their advantage to do so. Then Abd el-Kader would have to find some way to persuade them to renew their loyalty. The Berbers kept aloof in their mountainous strongholds, and the Arabs resented the Berbers, especially the very few who were part of Abd el-Kader's administration. And there was always distrust between urban and rural populations.

Recognizing that if the tribes offset each others' power, they would find it harder to unite against him, Abd el-Kader had to make inter-tribal rivalry work in his favor. Sometimes when a tribe refused to pay their taxes, for instance, or follow the Emir's leadership in battle, he had a rival tribe carry out punishment by the traditional means of raiding and pillaging.

THE COMPASSIONATE WARRIOR

THE SHAPE OF ABD EL-KADER'S STATE

Abd el-Kader did not try to encourage friendly relations, cooperation, and a sense of solidarity among the tribes. That would have been a hopeless task. Democracy and equality were not part of the state he envisaged at this stage. Rather, the tribes were governed by a hierarchy of officials, like a pyramid, with Abd el-Kader at the top. In effect, Abd el-Kader continued the "divide and rule" system of the old Ottoman government—all the while aiming at a unified society and a fair system of government. It was a very difficult balancing act.

In creating the administration of his state, it would have been natural for the Emir to choose men from his own class, the marabouts, because of their education and reputation for wisdom and virtue. But he realized that practical considerations must often outweigh principles. He chose many officials who had actually served under the Turks, because some continuity was important and their experience would be needed. At times a candidate's wealth and family connections would be more important than his ability and character. In general the Emir drew his officials from the elite classes, although from a much wider range of backgrounds—tribal, urban, religious—than had been true under Ottoman rule.

Abd el-Kader divided his territory into roughly equal parts called *khalifaliks*. At first there were four, and four more were added after the Treaty of Tafna had greatly expanded the Emir's territory. The man in charge of each *khalifalik* was a *khalifa*, like a "lieutenant governor." These were Abd el-Kader's right-hand men and most trusted advisers. They were responsible for collecting taxes, maintaining fighting troops, and handling complaints.

Each *khalifalik* was subdivided into *aghaliks*, which generally corresponded to the tribal divisions of land. They were all supposed to obey the same laws and follow the same administrative procedures. Abd el-Kader appointed the officials in charge of each level of administration: *khalifa*s, *agha*s, *qaid*s (chiefs at the tribal level), and *shaykh*s (chiefs of subdivisions within tribes). He also appointed judges, called *qadi*s, and aimed at a uniform, fair, and responsive judicial system. The *qadi*s were even given salaries—a new idea, intended to discourage corruption.

For the time and place, this administrative system was a radical concept. Previously, Algerian society had been a matter of each tribe for itself, with harsh discipline imposed by the regency government when things got out of hand.

RAISING MONEY FOR A NEW STATE

Traditional tribal society soon met further challenges. Abd el-Kader abolished the privileges of the powerful *makhzen* tribes, who had collected taxes from the *rayah*, "subject" tribes. This naturally angered the *makhzen* and encouraged them to collaborate with the French, but it pleased everyone else. At the same time, the Emir retained the basic system for collecting taxes. The principal tribe in each *aghalik* was designated as the new tax-collector, and these tribes became the new *makhzen* tribes. Since there were more of them, their power was spread more thinly and was less of a potential threat to the Emir's leadership.

Abd el-Kader took a pragmatic approach to taxation in another way as well. He abolished the much-resented tax imposed by the Ottoman government and replaced it with the traditional taxes specified under Islamic law. (These were the *zakat* tax in the spring, 3-4% of produce and other wealth, and the *ushr* in the fall, 10% of the grain.) In addition, when tribes submitted to the Emir's leadership and when administrative officials were appointed, they were expected to pay certain fees and send "gifts."

A strong, unified government needed much more income, and far more reliably, than just those taxes and gifts. Consequently, Abd el-Kader decided to set new taxes, which did *not* have a basis in religious law. Most important was a tax especially for fighting *jihad*, which he started levying in 1834. The *jihad* tax was collected during peace times as well as during war and became an essential source of income for the state.

But the tribes, much as they liked fighting *jihad*, hated having to pay for it. In general, they seized every opportunity to avoid paying the *jihad* tax, and Abd el-Kader, relying on the *khalifas'* forces, constantly had to keep after them. At one point he wrote to a French general, frankly revealing his frustrations:

> The Arab people are so constituted that if they had not seen [the *khalifa*'s powerful forces], they would have refused to pay the tax. After a success on your part [i.e., the French], how often did I encounter difficulties in gathering the contributions![1]

When hostilities did break out, some tribes reasoned that the Emir would be too busy to pay attention to them, so they could simply "forget" to pay their taxes—and take their chances on getting caught. Even under the best of conditions, the problem of inequality in taxation was a persistent problem. Some tribes paid little, especially those at the margins of the Emir's state and power, while others paid heavily.

Abd el-Kader's personal character and values served him well in the matter of taxation, as in so many other ways. He lived very simply and had no interest in ostentatious luxury or wealth. Thus he could convincingly claim that all the wealth collected as taxes and gifts went for the common good and not for his personal gain. That, too, was something new and revolutionary in the governance of Algeria.

CHAPTER 4: ABD EL-KADER'S VISION FOR HIS PEOPLE

FORMING AN ARMY

At the same time that these potentially far-reaching changes were taking shape, the Algerians could not forget that they were at war—or soon would be again. Indeed, building and maintaining a fighting force was the most pressing job of Abd el-Kader's state. He had to be able to count on a real army—not just the tribal warriors, who typically served for only a few days at a time. In fact, the tribal troops were not paid and had to provide their own food, weapons, and supplies. Little wonder that the Emir could not rely on them much.

In trying to establish an army, Abd el-Kader may well have been inspired by one of the experiences of his youth. When he and his father made their pilgrimage in the mid-1820s, stopping in Cairo for some time, they were welcomed by the ruler of Egypt, Muhammad Ali. This extraordinary individual, starting out as an Ottoman soldier stationed in Egypt, had seized power in 1805 in the most long-lasting revolution in modern Middle Eastern history. (His direct descendants ruled Egypt until 1952, when Egyptian army officers drove out the last king.) Aiming to create a strong state that could stand up to both the Ottoman Empire and the European states, Muhammad Ali had quickly introduced many reforms, especially affecting the military forces. His success in modernizing his army made a lasting impression on the visitors from Algeria.

Abd el-Kader, however, had to move even more quickly, building his state and his fighting force simultaneously. A strong army would have to be supported by a strong economy, so he encouraged agriculture, especially grain, which had a good market in Europe. His soldiers would need arms and other equipment, and he wanted to be as self-sufficient as possible. Therefore, he started a number of industrial operations on a modest scale, such as sawmills, tanneries, and forges,

THE COMPASSIONATE WARRIOR

often with help from Europeans. There was not enough time, though, for these attempts at modern technology to get off to a good start.

As for the army itself, Abd el-Kader maintained a corps of paid "lifetime" soldiers. Mostly infantry, their numbers ranged from around six thousand to as many as nine thousand five hundred men, according to various estimates. In addition he depended on a much larger number of cavalrymen and infantrymen from the tribes, where one of the *khalifas'* main duties was to keep troops ready to join the Emir's army when needed. Historians have estimated that at the height of his military buildup, in 1840, Abd el-Kader could command around seventy-five to eighty thousand men. In 1843 he wrote a booklet of rules, regulations, and standards for the army, with all promotions to be made by the Emir himself. The French were so impressed by this booklet that they translated it no fewer than six times.

During the period of peace under the Desmichels Treaty, the French military actually provided instruction for Abd el-Kader's army, plus uniforms, arms, and artillery. The Emir was happy to accept this help. Whatever military expertise he could acquire from his adversaries—who still regarded him as a valuable ally at that time—was a welcome boost to his own plans.

The military effectiveness of Abd el-Kader's army, however, was another matter. The concept of a regular, trained army was entirely new for the Algerians, who had had no military experience under the Ottomans. The Emir's uniformed and excellent horsemen looked very impressive; but when the commander of cavalry tried to persuade them to undergo training like that of the French cavalry, he got nowhere. They had complete confidence in their abilities as individual horsemen and fighters, but fighting as a unit was the last thing on their minds.

The Emir wanted a volunteer army. While his first calls attracted many young men, unfortunately, if not surprisingly, their enthusiasm for the soldier's life quickly faded. Before long he had to resort to conscription. The quality of soldiers and their preparation must have disappointed Abd el-Kader in the first years, but by 1839 the troops were reasonably well trained and equipped. With all its problems, the regular army proved the Emir's most effective means of extending and consolidating his control.

By the late 1830s, Abd el-Kader had laid the foundations of a new social organization and a state covering about two-thirds of the total territory of Algeria. While determined to make Islam the foundation for his government, he was a political thinker astute enough to know when and how to be flexible. He often faced problems and paradoxes that forced him to make decisions that he might not otherwise have chosen. The *jihad* tax was a good example: because the tax was resisted by the tribes, the Emir had to accept his French adversaries' help for his army—which would soon be fighting those very adversaries.

Even at its most successful, in 1838-39, Abd el-Kader's state was a loose creation, held together by little more than his own remarkable skills and by religion, especially the call for *jihad*. Many circumstances—the obstacles imposed by tribal society, the Algerians' lack of experience in self-government, the technologically more advanced invaders—worked against it. Yet, designed and set up in an extremely short time, his state was not only the first completely indigenous government in hundreds of years, but was also organized more fairly and run more humanely than any other government in North Africa and the Middle East at that time.

Even though Abd el-Kader's state lasted only a few years, his vision of new social and political possibilities was quite amazing. What might he have accomplished, in bringing his people into the fast-changing world of the nineteenth century, if he had really been able to pursue his dream of an ideal Islamic state?

CHAPTER 5

FRENCHMEN IN THE EMIR'S LIFE

While dealing with the weaknesses, needs, and potential of his own society, Abd el-Kader was also growing more aware of the nature of his adversaries—not just the French army's wanton cruelty but their apparent lack of religious faith. This was particularly baffling to him. How could a people consider themselves a great civilization if they had forgotten God?

But not all Frenchmen impressed him as irreligious. Three men who came into Abd el-Kader's life at this time, the late 1830s and early '40s, were individuals in whose lives religion played a vital part—in one way or another. These men, Léon Roches on the one hand, and the Bishop of Algiers and his assistant priest on the other, could not have been more different, nor could their stories have been a greater contrast. Yet all formed long and deep friendships with the Emir. These friendships, shaped in wartime, foreshadowed Abd el-Kader's ability to develop meaningful relationships with people of varied backgrounds, religious leanings, and moral qualities, which became such a striking aspect of his personality in later years.

THE COMPASSIONATE WARRIOR

LÉON ROCHES

A young cavalry lieutenant, Léon Roches taught himself Arabic so well that he soon became an official translator for the French army. In November of 1837, however, he decided to desert his post, find the Emir, and offer his services. That in itself was not extraordinary, as a few hundred other Europeans had already thrown in their lot with the Algerians. But Roches seems to have had a special objective. He was suffering from hopeless love for a young Algerian woman, and he dreamed that working with the Emir would somehow help him to find her again. Also, he seems to have been determined to lead as adventurous a life as humanly possible.

Once Abd el-Kader had assured himself that Roches was not a spy, he made the Frenchman his personal advisor and secretary. The two men soon had both a successful working relationship and a warm friendship. It was all the warmer because Roches said he had converted to Islam. His descriptions of Abd el-Kader in wide-ranging, sometimes contradictory moods, including what appeared to be spiritual exaltation, are among the most detailed and intimate of the many reports written about the Emir. "When he prays, he is an ascetic; when he commands, he is a sovereign; when he speaks of war, his features light up—he is a soldier."[1]

Roches' story sounds like a first-rate adventure film. Not long after he had joined the Emir's camp, for instance, he was forced to witness—without betraying even the slightest flicker of emotion—the swift beheading of captured tribal fighters who had resisted the Emir's campaign against their mountain stronghold. In that moment Roches saw the intense anger that Abd el-Kader was capable of—and the mercy that could just as quickly replace it.

The punishment of these men was an example of the Emir's ongoing struggle to keep the tribes with him. He knew that their loyalties could never be taken for granted, and he had to constantly impress them with his strength and control. It was largely for the same reason that Abd el-Kader undertook an astonishing campaign into the Sahara desert in June of 1838, an expedition that provided Léon Roches with all the adventure he could possibly have hoped for.

Abd el-Kader had received information that an important tribal leader named Muhammad at-Tijani was planning rebellion. The information was apparently false and maliciously intended, but Abd el-Kader was unaware of the deception and decided to deal with the matter seriously. The supposed troublemaker was also an esteemed marabout and head of a religious brotherhood. His palace, containing a fabulous treasure, was located inside a heavily fortified compound in an oasis called Ain Madhi, deep in the Sahara about two hundred miles south of Algiers. Abd el-Kader, in marching his army—possibly four or five thousand soldiers with their families, plus cavalry and artillery—for nearly three weeks through the desert, sent an unmistakable message. *Don't defy me—I will stop at nothing to subdue you.*

Why did the Emir undertake such a difficult and costly expedition? As he saw it, he had to bring Tijani's small but strategic town into the new state he was building, which he considered a religious as well as a political creation. It would not be right—or politically wise—to leave an important marabout outside. Furthermore, if the Emir should lose his towns and fortifications in the settled part of the country, he might need to fall back on a reliable base in the Sahara. And so he marched on, through summer heat.

When Abd el-Kader's army was near Ain Madhi, he sent a message demanding that Tijani accept his leadership. Tijani replied, denying any disloyalty but also flatly refusing to meet with the Emir. Abd el-Kader refused to accept such defiance and began a European-style siege that lasted more than four months. During the standoff, he had time to send for cannons, explosives, and other equipment for siege—some provided by the French. But how to determine the strength of those walls?

Léon Roches promptly volunteered to get inside—or die in the attempt. Reluctantly, Abd el-Kader allowed him to try. Roches managed to get inside and even spoke to Tijani in person. He returned unharmed to Abd el-Kader, with vital information about the fortifications—and Tijani's continued defiance.

Abd el-Kader gave orders to dig tunnels under the walls. This went on for much of the summer and occasionally produced bloody encounters with the defenders. Finally, deceived by a possible ruse, Tijani gave up. With all his people and his treasure, he agreed to leave, pay the Emir's expenses for the whole campaign, and make no further trouble. When the fort was empty, Abd el-Kader had it blown up. But it seems to have been a wasted victory, because as soon as Abd el-Kader was busy with war again, Tijani returned, rebuilt his fort, and went over to the French.

In any event, Roches' close friendship with the Emir continued. In spite of the jealousy of others in the camp, Abd el-Kader increasingly relied on the Frenchman as the likelihood of resumed warfare grew closer. Not only did Roches translate French newspapers and documents and write the Emir's communications with the French, but he made significant improvements in managing the army and the tribes.

Then came a dark evening at the end of October 1839, when Abd el-Kader learned that outbreak of war was almost imminent. To the Emir's surprise, Roches reacted with obvious sadness. Overcome by torn loyalties, he could not face actual warfare against his own countrymen—and at last he told Abd el-Kader the truth. He had *not* converted to Islam, he was still a Christian. He was willing to pay the ultimate price for his deception, but he could no longer conceal the reality.

Abd el-Kader was stunned. He begged and pleaded, stormed and denounced. Finally he drove Roches from his tent. A few days later, sick with fever, Roches managed to escape to French lines—very probably because the Emir had purposely allowed him to slip away. At first Roches was treated with suspicion, but before long the French generals were satisfied that he was not a spy. With his knowledge of Arabic he soon became one of Bugeaud's right-hand men and an invaluable source of information for the French general's campaigns.

Remarkably, the painful break was *not* the end of this relationship, and Léon Roches would reappear in the Emir's story.

BISHOP DUPUCH AND FATHER SUCHET

One day in the spring of 1841, when intense fighting had resumed, Abd el-Kader received a letter from the Bishop of Algiers, Antoine-Adolphe Dupuch. The bishop had been approached by a woman asking his assistance in obtaining release of her husband, a prisoner of the Emir's forces. Dupuch, who could never resist a call for help, decided to write directly to the Emir.

Abd el-Kader, a master of persuasion, wrote back. He had heard much about the bishop's humanity and Christian charity, he said; but why ask for the release of only one man? Why not *all* the French prisoners? And for that matter, why not release an equal number of Algerian prisoners, many of them innocent villagers? The bishop thought a prisoner exchange was a fine idea. As he explained it to the French generals, it would advance the cause not only of French civilization but of Christianity, through noble example. The French generals were not at all impressed, but grudgingly they gave permission to proceed.

THE COMPASSIONATE WARRIOR

Bishop Dupuch, after seeing to it that the Muslim prisoners were given decent clothes, designated another priest, Father Jacques Suchet, to carry out the prisoner exchange. A troop of one hundred and thirty Algerian civilians set out on May 17, 1841, for a certain location. The women and children rode in rented carriages, the men walked, and the prisoner exchange succeeded. The Algerian prisoners reported favorably on the bishop's kindness toward them. An exchange of gifts sealed the agreement: a clock and two candelabras for the Algerians, a herd of goats for the bishop.

There were more French prisoners, however. Dupuch wanted to free them, too, and again Father Suchet agreed to take on the job. This time he had to go deep into hostile territory and try to meet the Emir himself. He took with him a quantity of medical supplies, knowing they were always needed among the tribes.

Upon meeting Abd el-Kader's representative, Suchet was treated courteously but told that no one had any idea where the Emir might be found. It was very probably true. An essential part of the Emir's war plan was to keep constantly on the move, covering an immense territory. A young Algerian guide was assigned to the priest, and they spent several days vigorously hiking from one place to another. At long last, somewhere near Mascara they found Abd el-Kader, sitting under a fig tree.

The priest, like so many other Europeans who actually met the Emir, was surprised at his mild appearance and quiet manner. Official propaganda, of course, had described him as a fierce and bloodthirsty barbarian. Abd el-Kader welcomed Suchet and expressed appreciation for the kindness toward the Algerian prisoners. The two men sat together under the tree and negotiated, using the Emir's interpreter. Abd el-Kader agreed to release some fifty additional French prisoners, even without an equal number of Algerian prisoners in exchange.

42

CHAPTER 5: FRENCHMEN IN THE EMIR'S LIFE

Then they started talking about what really interested the Emir: religious faith.

While growing up, Abd el-Kader had learned something about other religions from books, but he had not known any Christians until the French invasion—which had initially seemed to him like a "crusade," an attack on Islam. As he met more Frenchmen, he was learning more about Christianity, for better and worse. Now he welcomed the chance to talk with a devout and knowledgeable Christian, for there were certain questions that puzzled him.

For instance, the divine nature of Jesus Christ—a basic question, because Muslims esteem Jesus as a prophet but do not believe he was of the same nature as God. Abd el-Kader also wanted to understand the purpose of Catholic priests better. Suchet said that their ministry was to treat all men, regardless of religion, as brothers. But why, asked Abd el-Kader, didn't all Frenchmen observe the beliefs of their religion? Suchet answered with the same question: why didn't all Muslims observe the teachings of *their* religion? Abd el-Kader could only imply that he agreed. His fellow Muslims' ignorance of true Islam was a constant grief to him.

At the end of this difficult but surprisingly fruitful expedition, Suchet brought Bishop Dupuch a glowing report. Prisoners-of-war would be allowed to write to their families, and the Emir had even agreed to allow Catholic priests to stay with French prisoners.

But Suchet's report was as far as the two priests got with their good intentions. Again Bugeaud and his generals stepped in and put a stop to ideas about treating humanely with the enemy. No priests for prisoners, no softening of Bugeaud's policy of brute force and destruction, absolutely no further communication with the Emir. War was a grim business. It would be demoralizing for French troops to accept the idea that the Algerians and their leader were good people. Much better to think of them as monsters to be feared, hated, and ultimately destroyed.

CHAPTER 6

WAR OF TOTAL CONQUEST

Early in 1839, Abd el-Kader wrote a surprising letter to the Sultan of Morocco. His people, he said, were finally united and lawful—so much so that "a young girl could cross the country alone, east to west, night or day, without fear of a single bad encounter."[1]

By the fall of 1839, however, both French and Algerians were itching to start fighting again. What had happened—and why would either side have preferred the horrors of war to even the uneasy peace achieved by the Tafna Treaty?

The moment of optimism had passed. Abd el-Kader knew that if he held to the truce in hopes of gaining strength, his adversary would surely grow even stronger. European settlers were arriving all the time and seizing the Algerians' land. The most compelling reason for renewing hostilities, however, was that delay would undermine Abd el-Kader's own strength. His councilors kept reminding him that he must revive the call for *jihad*, or the tribes would not stay with him. And why should they have to pay the special *jihad* tax if they weren't fighting *jihad*? Some tribal leaders even thought Abd el-Kader's treaty with the French, which looked more like an alliance, made him a poor leader of *jihad*.

The interlude of peace had given Abd el-Kader time to start on his grand plan of revitalizing his people and forming a unified state. But if the tribes defected and made their own peace with the French, his Algerian state would soon disintegrate. He would have to set aside that goal for a while and take direct action against the invaders.

The French, meanwhile, were still debating the basic question: should they limit their control to a few coastal towns plus some settlements on interior plains near Algiers—or go all-out and take the whole country? Voices for the latter choice were growing louder.

Then fresh scandal erupted over the Tafna Treaty. The French government had always disliked the treaty because it gave Abd el-Kader so much territory, and now secret provisions revealed that thanks to the Emir's skillful bargaining, France had given away even more. Abd el-Kader would be supplied with a large quantity of rifles and gunpowder, and in return he would give General Bugeaud a considerable sum of money. The government in Paris was starting to wonder whether the Emir really needed all those arms *only* to keep the tribes in line. Or, with his increasingly impressive army, could he actually be preparing for renewed war with France? Maybe it was time to scrap that treaty.

THE START OF ALL-OUT WAR

Both sides, therefore, wanted to bring about a crisis, a cause for war. The opportunity lay in the vague language of the Tafna Treaty. Although in effect this treaty gave Abd el-Kader control of about two-thirds of the entire country, it reserved for France the territory around Algiers extending to a point "above" a certain river. Or did the Arabic word in question mean "beyond" that river, as the French argued? Abd el-Kader could not accept the French interpretation, because "beyond" the river would mean the entire country to the east.

Nothing came of either side's efforts to solve this confusion. Abd el-Kader even wrote to the French king—one of the last services that Léon Roches performed for him.

In October of 1839, Governor-General Valée decided on a test. He would send a contingent of soldiers overland from Constantine to Algiers. For the French, this was a logical way to develop contact between the inland city of Constantine, recently captured, and the capital city on the coast. The French soldiers' route, however, went through territory that Abd el-Kader considered under *his* control. If the French thought they could march through his territory without his permission, wouldn't they try to claim all the land between Constantine and Algiers?

Abd el-Kader wrote a sharp protest, to which Valée answered that the excursion was nothing important, little more than a pleasant outing. In a second message, Abd el-Kader took a different tack. He did not want war, he explained, but his councilors were all calling for *jihad* and he had to obey religious law in such matters.

Having warned the French and sought legal counsel, Abd el-Kader then took action: well planned, sudden, and lethal. In November his army attacked the Mitidja plain south of Algiers, where a European population had settled. Many lives were lost and virtually all the homes and farms destroyed. The war was on.

This campaign brought the Emir the closest he ever came to driving the French back to the sea. In 1840 the tribes were fully behind him, he could command about 80,000 men, and he was at the height of his power. It was still an uneven fight, as the French had at least as many soldiers, much better trained, and many more in reserve. Nonetheless, with Abd el-Kader's forces attacking European settlements around Algiers, Oran, and Titteri province, the French government grew alarmed. Valée's counter-offensive did not produce results quickly enough to satisfy Paris, and he was relieved of his duties as governor-general in December of 1840. His replacement in early 1841 was General Bugeaud.

This was the tough, campaign-hardened, opinionated Bugeaud who had signed the Tafna Treaty with Abd el-Kader in 1837. At that time, he had praised the Emir to the skies: honest, competent, reliable, just the man with whom France could work out territorial arrangements that would suit both sides. Furthermore, in 1837 Bugeaud was still only half-hearted about the French presence in Algeria. What really interested him was upgrading the roads and bridges of his home province in France! That was how he intended to use the money secretly promised under the treaty.

By the time Bugeaud returned to Algeria as governor-general, however, his views had turned around completely. Now he was all for full-scale war and a thoroughly French Algeria. France should quickly clear away the native people, so that Algerian soil could be populated with European colonists. Only the French flag would fly in Algeria. Under Bugeaud's leadership, the debate was settled at last. He immediately undertook a vigorous, aggressive, no-holds-barred military strategy that earned him a decidedly mixed reputation.

At the top of Bugeaud's instructions from the French government was the specific order to get rid of Abd el-Kader. The Emir, at first unaware that he was the main target, sent conciliatory messages, but it soon became evident that Bugeaud had other plans.

BUGEAUD'S WAR

As 1841 progressed, the war took on a terrible nature. In the early years of the conquest, the French had destroyed cities and massacred their

48

populations. Now they turned the same tactics upon the rural people. They raided villages, destroying and killing; they cut down olive groves and fruit orchards, burned fields of grain. In summer they made the term "scorched earth" an all-too-accurate description of the Algerian countryside. In winter they drove people from their homes to die of cold in the mountains. They learned how to find the peasants' stores of grain hidden in large containers underground by systematically walking along and prodding the ground with their bayonets until they hit the tell-tale stone lids.

It was a war waged on a *people*, not on a state or army. Bugeaud's objectives were to make life virtually impossible for the rural people, and at the same time to turn the tribes away from Abd el-Kader. Tribes were compelled to fight against the Emir under threat of being deported to distant French possessions in the Caribbean and the South Pacific. French strategy not only demoralized the Algerian people but disrupted the whole economy of the country. The destruction of rural life cut off both the income and the military intelligence that Abd el-Kader needed to continue the fight.

Meanwhile, Bugeaud brought about major changes in the French army and its methods of warfare. Earlier, the soldiers had been sent out in armies of several thousands, as in European campaigns, each man heavily burdened with his equipment, bedding, and food. They had to drag heavy cannons and baggage wagons wherever they went—not to mention wearing tight woolen uniforms in the desert heat. They dropped along the way from sickness, exhaustion, and suicide. For this recklessly conceived adventure, France paid a huge price in the suffering and sacrifice of its own men.

One reason Bugeaud had wanted the time-out provided by the Tafna Treaty was to undertake major reorganization of the army. He created much smaller contingents of soldiers that could move swiftly through the countryside, without heavy artillery and other equipment. When war resumed, the "flying columns" were much more successful in carrying out destructive sorties against the tribes and villages.

The French army reflected local realities in another way as well. Starting as early as 1831, it included a few companies of indigenous soldiers: the *zouaves*, light infantry, and the *spahis*, light cavalry. The *zouaves* were mostly Berbers from the Kabyle mountains and thus somewhat separate from the main population of Arabs. Both *spahis* and *zouaves* wore colorful uniforms, bright red and blue—and this fact would play an important role in one of the major crises of the whole war.

Looking ahead, Bugeaud had ambitious plans for his military. Expecting that the tribes would all ultimately submit to France but would never really be loyal, he decided that France would run the country with its army. French soldiers would police the tribes through a military administration, and also build the roads and bridges that would encourage more Europeans to come. Before long, Bugeaud predicted, the Algerians would see that the "wheel of fortune" now definitely favored the Europeans—and would never turn their way again.

ABD EL-KADER'S WAR

Like any military leader, Abd el-Kader did what he thought *had* to be done to achieve his objectives, no matter how much he might have preferred not to take actions that were ruthless or deceptive. But whenever possible he tried to prevent brutality, and he demanded a remarkably high standard of behavior from his followers.

From the start of his command, the Emir had deplored the savage traditions of tribal warfare. At the battle of the Macta River in June 1835, the first major loss for the French, he had been horrified to see piles of severed French heads. Yet he knew that making changes too quickly would alienate the tribes. Therefore, he enforced new rules gradually but with firm discipline, and it usually took only a few examples of harsh punishment, such as heavy beatings, to get the message across.

As for strategy, Abd el-Kader was well aware that pitched battles would never work. He had fought in this way only once, in July of 1836 at the Sikkak River, and his army had been crushed. The French were too strong in numbers, disciplined training, and arms. Guerilla warfare was the only way: harassing the enemy, cutting supply and communications lines, attacking without warning and disappearing just as quickly.

For a few years Abd el-Kader held lines of defense—major towns and fortifications—running roughly east and west. All were lost to the French army, however, by the end of 1841. In most cases the inhabitants had been warned to leave in time, so the French found only empty streets and buildings.

What about allies, or help from outside? In the spring of 1840, soon after the French counter-offensive, the Emir sought help from Britain and even from the Ottoman sultan; both refused. He continued to obtain arms from Britain through Morocco, but his relations with the Moroccan sultan were getting worse. Without bases, limited to guerilla warfare with only partially dependable fighters, Abd el-Kader was on his own against a military superpower, possibly the strongest modern army in the world at that time.

Psychologically as well as militarily, however, guerilla warfare could be highly effective. Since the Emir and his army could move so swiftly on horseback through both the countryside and rugged mountainous areas, the war became a cat-and-mouse affair. The French certainly tried, but they could never quite catch Abd el-Kader. He would evade, escape, cover seemingly impossible distances in a night, strike a target, and vanish. Bugeaud complained that to find Abd el-Kader he needed a magician, and the soldiers needed wings to catch him. At the same time, the Algerians could not inflict blows hard enough to stop the relentless progress of the French army.

But the Emir's men did have military successes, and they took French prisoners—who had been told by their officers that their fate, if captured, would be worse than horrible. What the prisoners actually experienced is one of the most interesting aspects of Abd el-Kader's whole military career. Although the war was bitter and bloody, the Emir was careful to treat all prisoners properly. It was a matter of policy, religion, and human values for him. Indeed, he enjoyed talking with the captives, especially the well educated officers, and learning more about the people and country who had become his enemy.

Abd el-Kader's insistence on decent treatment of prisoners was not only humane but wise strategy, as it undermined French propaganda intended to stiffen soldiers' determination to fight to the death. In trying to set humane standards, he provided a model for later international conventions on treatment of prisoners-of-war.

European women, too, were sometimes taken prisoner. Some were women who managed canteens for the armies in the field, others were from the settlements. Abd el-Kader put his mother, the hardworking and capable Lalla Zohra, in charge of the women, and she saw to it that they were fed, clothed, and protected against possible abuse. Lalla Zohra also took it upon herself to look after sick and wounded French prisoners.

All this time, Abd el-Kader had to fight on two fronts: against the French, and against the fragmented nature of tribal society. From

1840-42 the tribes could see that he was carrying on *jihad*, and they supported him. That is, they would be loyal until the French military put them under too much pressure. Whenever a tribe defected, Abd el-Kader had to weigh carefully the particular circumstances. Was the tribe weak-willed, opportunistic? Then they probably deserved punishment by raiding. Or had they resisted until they were exhausted and had no resources left? In that case the Emir's response would be much milder.

What soon became devastatingly clear, however, was the fate of Abd el-Kader's unified Algerian state. As the war went on, the cities that might have served as his political capitals—Mascara, Tagdempt, Tlemcen—all fell to the French. Even the small village of Guetna and its *zawiya*, where Abd el-Kader had grown up, was deliberately destroyed as a blow to his morale. Likewise, the towns that served as the *khalifas'* headquarters and depots for supplies had to be abandoned. Abd el-Kader's state simply disintegrated. One can only imagine his emotions as he observed the vanishing of his dream. With it went all hope of an authentic Algerian state for more than a hundred years.

THE *SMALA*, ABD EL-KADER'S "FLOATING CAPITAL"

Although the Emir had to be constantly on the move, toward the end of 1842 he created a new means of holding his people together. This was the *smala*—literally "household"—a tent city that housed the Emir's army and their families. It also housed tribes who had joined him, refugees from destroyed towns and villages, prisoners-of-war, French deserters, hostages from tribes being disciplined, and more. Since the people needed their livestock for food, the *smala* included tens of thousands of animals as well.

The *smala* set up schools, workshops, markets and bazaars, mosques, everything needed to keep a society going. Abd el-Kader's mother han-

THE COMPASSIONATE WARRIOR

dled the finances, mostly for purchase of grain, and Algerian Jews loyal
to the Emir provided for the destitute.

The tents of the *smala* were carefully arranged in several concentric
circles. The Emir's family was in the center, his *khalifa*s and their families in the first circle, and so on, with the tribes and common people
on the outside. By early 1842, sixty or seventy thousand people were
living in the *smala*, and at times possibly more. It became a sort of
"floating capital," because whenever necessary, the whole collection of
tents—hundreds of them—could be dismantled, moved, and set up
again somewhere else in the same order.

Unfortunately this became necessary quite often, as Abd el-Kader
and his people always had to keep hiding from the French. Although the
smala had to serve as the center of his political power, its unstable, nomadic nature was inevitably demoralizing. Wherever the *smala* settled,
moreover, the concentration of people and animals nearly wrecked the
environment. The sheep, goats, horses, camels, and donkeys needed a
great deal of water and often reduced water sources to muddy holes.
Sickness spread quickly. Abd el-Kader appointed officials to try to protect the land and water sources, but it was a losing struggle.

As soon as the French generals learned about the *smala*, they gave
top priority to finding it. "Flying columns" went out frequently and in
all directions, according to a regular plan.

In May of 1843 a mobile unit of about five hundred soldiers under the command of the king's twenty-one-year-old son, the Duke of
Aumale, went out searching. Suddenly—almost by accident—they discovered the tent city spread out before them. The people of the *smala*
were frantically busy setting up in a new location. Seeing the bright red
cloaks of the *spahi*s, the indigenous cavalrymen in the French army,
they at first thought that Abd el-Kader's men—who also wore red uni-

forms—were returning. They sent up loud cheers of welcome. By the time they realized that the approaching soldiers were the enemy—and a very small number at that—it was too late. The French easily demolished the entire *smala*.

Abd el-Kader, who was elsewhere at the time, learned of the catastrophe a few days later. His own family had been spirited to safety, but three thousand prisoners, all the livestock, and the entire treasury had been taken. And—what especially stunned the marabout-warrior—his library of some five thousand precious manuscripts had been totally burned and scattered to the winds.

FRENCH CONQUEST ACCOMPLISHED?

The heartbreaking destruction of Abd el-Kader's *smala* was a turning point in the whole campaign of resistance. For at least a year and a half, the Algerians' fortunes were low. Abd el-Kader set up a much smaller "floating capital," actually just a large camp, and moved it to safety in Morocco—where the Algerians were never really welcome. His army remained in Algeria under the command of one of his most trusted *khalifa*s, Ben Allal.

By the end of 1843, Bugeaud and his generals were rejoicing, confident that the war was nearly won. The fight against Abd el-Kader had become largely a man-hunt, and the French columns pursued him relentlessly. Although he always managed to elude them, barely escaping with his life on at least two occasions, they clearly had him on the run. In November the Emir's *khalifa*, Ben Allal—respected by the French generals as well as the tribal leaders—was killed in a battle. To further demoralize the tribes and villages, the French displayed his severed head widely for days. Then Bugeaud ordered a burial with military honors.

The French established military control over the areas that they had pacified, up to the northern edge of the Sahara. Bugeaud—who always admired Abd el-Kader—kept the basic organization of the countryside that the Emir had created in his short-lived state. Muslim officials were appointed, but the French military held the power. More and more Europeans were settling on lands seized from the tribes. The military administration weighed heavily on the impoverished and exhausted Algerians . . . and underneath, anger was coming to a boil.

CHAPTER 7

THE DEVASTATING TIDES OF WAR

Suddenly the war took another turn, in some ways downright bizarre. For the first time in several years, Abd el-Kader was challenged as leader of the Algerians' resistance.

ALGERIAN RIVALS—AND FRENCH BRUTALITIES

Early in 1845, in a mountain village near the coast, a young man announced that God had appointed him to drive out the infidels. This man soon became known as Bou Maza (which could be translated "the man with the goat") because his pet goat, he claimed, conveyed God's messages to him. The rural people, oppressed and disheartened, yet inspired by traditional beliefs in "saints," eagerly followed the charismatic new leader.

Described as unusually handsome, Bou Maza had the appearance of a mystic but was nevertheless a ruthless fighter. Starting by butchering some Muslim officials appointed by the French, for several months he led a widespread insurrection in the countryside. His success inspired a whole wave of "Goat men" who took the same name and tactics, and soon insurgencies were cropping up everywhere and keeping the central part of the country in turmoil.

Abd el-Kader faced an awkward situation. His own campaign, insofar as possible, had been organized and disciplined. In contrast, Bou Maza was a violent bandit. Should Abd el-Kader oppose this rival, or find some way to work with him? The French, on the defensive, were afraid that if Abd el-Kader should join forces with these insurgencies, recently pacified tribes might try to switch back to the Emir. Meanwhile, the revived resistance gave Abd el-Kader the chance to strengthen his camp—still in Morocco—and build up his army again.

For a brief time Bou Maza joined Abd el-Kader's camp, but it was not a friendly alliance and he soon left. He surrendered to the French in April 1847 and was taken to Paris—where, thanks to his charisma, he became a society idol! Eventually he went to fight in the Crimean War (1853-56), and there his story appears to have ended. The other "Goat men" faded away.

While putting down the Bou Maza insurrection, however, the French army committed atrocities that gave an indelibly horrific stain to their actions in Algeria. In Dahra, a mountainous region full of caves, a large number of tribespeople took refuge in an extensive, many-chambered cavern. When the French officer in charge, Pélissier, could not persuade them to surrender, he had the entrances to the cave system blocked with wood and brush, and set on fire. Possibly as many as a thousand men, women, and children died of suffocation, along with their animals.

Pélissier's report produced outrage in France. Thereafter, although at least three similar atrocities were carried out, killing many hundreds of people, the French officers tried to keep quiet about it. Governor-General Bugeaud did not explicitly order his army to carry out such acts, but he openly approved them. So hardened had many officers and soldiers become by then, that shocking displays of cruelty seem to have been brushed off. But public opinion in France and elsewhere in Europe was horrified.

THE EMIR'S RESPONSE

The Bou Maza insurrections and the French brutalities helped spur Abd el-Kader into action again. In the fall of 1845 he returned to Algeria from Morocco with six thousand cavalry and renewed support from many tribes. For several months he moved swiftly across the country, sometimes riding fifty miles in a night. His goal was to reach the Kabyle Mountains in the eastern part of the country and help his Berber *khalifa* galvanize the local tribes into *jihad*.

Throughout the bitterly harsh winter of 1845-46 the cat-and-mouse game went on. The French lost three generals to cold and exhaustion, plus men counted in the hundreds, and horses in the thousands. Abd el-Kader was here, there, and at times it seemed everywhere. Catching Abd el-Kader was once more the foremost objective of the French army, and every French general wanted that honor.

In Great Britain, never very sympathetic regarding French imperial ambitions, the press fired up. What? The "Butcher of the Bedouins"—their name for Bugeaud—couldn't catch one man? Maybe that man didn't even exist! The satirical British journal *Punch* described Bugeaud's efforts in a rollicking long poem entitled "Catching Abd-el-Kader." Here's a sample.

> He made the most perfect arrangements
> For catching him 'ere he started,
> But whenever he got
> To a suitable spot,
> Abd-el-Kader had just departed.

THE COMPASSIONATE WARRIOR

> There was great expectation in Paris,
> But to the war minister's sorrow,
> The telegraph's tale
> Ran thus, without fail,
> "The capture's put off till to-morrow."
>
> France won victories by dozens—
> And each day, as the marshal [Bugeaud] strode on,
> We were sure to hear
> That they'd missed the Emir,
> But killed the horse he rode on.[1]

Americans, too, were fascinated by the courageous leader of a doomed fight for freedom. In the Midwest, a man who had been eagerly following the British press reports decided to name a new town in honor of the Emir. That town is Elkader, Iowa, which has always taken great pride in its historical connection with Abd el-Kader.

Constantly pursued, the Emir was saved from capture several times by tribal people who provided intelligence about French moves. But it was getting harder and harder for him to keep the tribes' active support. They were exhausted and discouraged, and they feared punishment by the French army. With an army of one hundred and six thousand, the generals sent their flying columns after the Emir so persistently that by the summer of 1846 he was again forced to seek refuge in Morocco.

THE SIDI BRAHIM INCIDENT AND TRAGIC AFTERMATH

Since Abd el-Kader's warfare was based on guerilla tactics, very few encounters stand out in the historical record. One incident, however, during the renewed campaign that started in the fall of 1845, was memorable. Characterized by foolhardy thinking, bravery, and suffering on the French side, it had drastic after-effects for the Emir.

CHAPTER 7: THE DEVASTATING TIDES OF WAR

Near the border between Algeria and Morocco, the French had a garrison at a small port called Djemaa Ghazaouet—"the pirates' base." The officer in charge was Lieutenant Colonel Montagnac, courageous, ambitious, and tough—to a fault. In September of 1845, he learned that Abd el-Kader and his men were nearby in the steep hills close to the coast. Fed up with a waiting game that asked so little of him, Montagnac decided—against orders—to set off with four hundred and twenty-five men to seek action. In a narrow ravine they ran into a deadly ambush, which killed Montagnac and many of his men. About eighty of the remaining soldiers scrambled along the sides of the ravine to take shelter in a small religious shrine known as Sidi Brahim.

So confident of success had Montagnac been when he set out, that he and his men had not brought food or even water with them. They were besieged in the shrine for two days, all the while defying Abd el-Kader's appeals for surrender. Finally, desperate from thirst, the French soldiers tried to dash back the twelve miles to their fort by the sea. Only seventeen of the original four hundred and twenty-five managed to reach safety. Ninety-seven were captured, and the rest all killed.

The prisoners were taken to Abd el-Kader's camp, the remains of the "floating capital," in Morocco. Soon, about two hundred more French soldiers, captured from an ambushed supply column, joined them. Conditions were extremely difficult in the camp. With nowhere near enough food or shelter, everyone suffered, Algerians and prisoners alike. Bugeaud refused repeated offers of a prisoner exchange, saying it would be exploited as a sign of French weakening.

Abd el-Kader was away and constantly on the move in Algeria. He had left his brother-in-law, Ben Thami, in charge of the camp, along with the trusted *khalifa* Bou Hamidi. The winter months dragged on, provisions grew even scarcer, and the two men argued about how to handle the problem. Bou Hamidi wanted to release the prisoners, as he believed Abd el-Kader would have done. Ben Thami disagreed. On an April night in 1846, Ben Thami made his decision. He had the French officers taken to a place of safety, leaving the ordinary soldiers in their tents. Then all the soldiers, possibly as many as two hundred men, were killed.

When he learned of the massacre, Abd el-Kader was utterly dismayed. This was not his way—killing defenseless prisoners-of-war in cold blood! It was a terrible blow to his rules of war, his standards of humane behavior, his very reputation. Yet as the Commander, he had to take responsibility for the whole matter. In France, the outcry was now against the supposed treachery and cruelty of the Emir. Popular support swung back to Bugeaud and his war of complete conquest. The ugly accusation against Abd el-Kader would haunt him for years.

THE SULTAN OF MOROCCO: PARTNER OR RIVAL?

Abd el-Kader now had to deal with a third adversary besides the French army and the shifting tribal alliances: the Sultan of Morocco, Abd ar-Rahman. With the passing years, the sultan had come to regard Abd el-Kader as a threat because so many Moroccans admired him and wanted to join in the Algerians' *jihad*. The French demanded that the sultan not support Abd el-Kader; and the British, who wanted to prevent any excuse for the French to invade Morocco, also put pressure on him. Therefore, while the sultan reluctantly allowed Abd el-Kader to seek safety for himself, his army, and his camp on Moroccan soil, there was no friendship involved.

In the spring of 1844, the Emir's popularity with the Moroccan people forced the sultan to send troops to help the Algerians. As a result, a confrontation arose between Morocco and France. Bugeaud invaded Morocco in August and defeated a much larger Moroccan army, led by a boastful but inexperienced son of the sultan. The humiliating defeat turned Sultan Abd ar-Rahman completely against the Algerians, and he signed a treaty with the French declaring Abd el-Kader an outlaw.

In 1846, as his campaign in Algeria was dwindling to a standstill, Abd el-Kader had to retreat to Morocco once more. But Moroccan soil was hardly a refuge, and now his army and camp became the sultan's target. Moroccan soldiers destroyed two of the largest Algerian tribes still loyal to Abd el-Kader, which severely undermined his support in both Morocco and Algeria.

ABD EL-KADER AGAINST A WALL

In hopes of avoiding an all-out war with the sultan, in November of 1847 Abd el-Kader sent his trusted *khalifa* Bou Hamidi to the sultan's capital for negotiations. By this time, most of the *khalifa*s had been killed or captured, and Abd el-Kader's hopes rested heavily on Bou Hamidi. But instead of being treated as a respected official, Bou Hamidi was thrown in jail and forced to drink a lethal dose of poison. Abd el-Kader knew that he would have to get his people out of Morocco as quickly as possible.

In mid-December of 1847, he managed to evade the Moroccan army and move his whole camp across the river that marked the boundary between Moroccan and Algerian territory. They were now safer, but their situation was no less dire. The army's ranks were depleted, the tribes were fast drifting away, the families in the camp were hungry and weak. And the French positions in western Algeria were by now so strong that the Emir could see no chance for further action against them.

Abd el-Kader was virtually trapped. His two choices became stark indeed. He might leave his camp behind, escape into the interior, rally what forces he could, and go on with the struggle. That was what most of his advisers were urging him to do. Or he might stay with his people, and give in to the French. For a leader of *jihad*, which would be the more honorable course to take? And how, in this dilemma, should honor be defined?

CHAPTER 8

PROMISES KEPT AND BROKEN

On the stormy night of December 22, 1847, the wind blustered so fiercely that Abd el-Kader could hardly hold the paper on which he was trying to write. Finally he just attached his seal to the piece of paper and gave it to the young messenger, along with a verbal request to the French general for a safe-conduct guarantee.

The two armies were both in the high hills about twenty miles from the westernmost coast of Algeria. But their positions were vastly different. General August Lamoricière was confidently leading a column of soldiers toward a nearby pass that he wanted to secure. Abd el-Kader, cut off from any chance of a successful attack, had finally made his decision.

ABD EL-KADER'S DECISION

Back and forth between the two camps, through rain and wind, rode the emissary for the French. In his second message, Abd el-Kader stated his terms for yielding. He would completely cease his struggle against the French and leave Algeria forever, on condition that he, his family, and supporters could live in a predominantly Muslim city in either Egypt or Palestine. General Lamoricière wrote a prompt reply, promising to meet the Emir's terms.

Reassured, Abd el-Kader and about sixty-five of his men set out for the French fort at Djemaa Ghazaouet, the "pirates' base." Near the shrine of Sidi Brahim—the very place where, two years earlier, they had inflicted such a terrible blow on the enemy—they encountered French cavalry. This time, however, there was no shooting. Nor was there any of the mocking or humiliating spectacle that Abd el-Kader had feared might take place. Instead, the five hundred French cavalrymen in two rows saluted Abd el-Kader as he rode past. He stopped briefly at the shrine to pray, and then rode on to the French fort.

On the way, the Emir met Lamoricière, a man of both military competence and social conscience, who had campaigned against Abd el-Kader for years. Dismounting, he handed the general his sword. When the Emir ordered his men to lay down their arms, however, Lamoricière told them to keep their weapons. They would be welcome henceforth, he said, to serve France.

Soon after Abd el-Kader reached the fort, he found that the Duke of Aumale, son of the French king, had also arrived. In spite of the bad weather, the prince had come as quickly as possible by ship from Oran to meet Abd el-Kader and accept his surrender. This was the very officer who, back in the spring of 1843, had discovered the Emir's "floating capital," the *smala*, and utterly destroyed it.

The next morning the Duke reviewed his troops. Abd el-Kader remarked on the contrast between their exemplary training and the undisciplined fighting style of his own men. He offered the Duke his black mare, the last horse he had ridden in battle, and the prince accepted the gift graciously, promising in turn to protect the Emir and his people.

All this while, the French officers and soldiers at the fort were celebrating their victory. At last they had defeated their arch-enemy, the notorious Emir Abd el-Kader! They had caught the wily adversary who had forced them into such a long, costly struggle, for fifteen blood-soaked years! Every officer in the French army had long dreamed of receiving the surrender of the Emir and his stubborn Algerians—and *they*, the men at the lonely "gathering-place of pirates," were the ones to have that honor.

Sitting quietly in the tent provided to him, Abd el-Kader looked at the matter differently. He knew he could have escaped to the south and gone on with the war somehow, but he had decided otherwise. He would stop leading the resistance at a time and place of his own choosing, based on his calculation of the suffering that his people, who had already suffered so much, would have to endure. He believed that this was the better course for everyone. From his viewpoint, therefore, it was not a matter of "surrender" or "giving up," let alone "being caught." Rather, it was a deliberate choice to put an end to the struggle and move on to a radically different life, the life that he regarded as his true calling.

And there was one other reason, most important of all. His decision, Abd el-Kader believed, was made according to God's will. He was now convinced that God had decided for Algeria to be governed by France, a Christian nation. He, the Emir Abd el-Kader, was only the servant of the Almighty—the literal meaning of his name, in fact. He must accept God's decision. This underlying conviction helps explain much of the Emir's attitudes and actions for the rest of his life.

ABD EL-KADER AT TOULON

Most brief historical accounts of the years after Abd el-Kader stopped fighting state simply that he was "imprisoned," or kept in "French prisons." This gives a very misleading impression of what actually happened. The story of Abd el-Kader's treatment in France is in some ways as dramatic as the story of his many years of resistance in his homeland. It's a story of frustration and determination on Abd el-Kader's part; and on the part of the French government, one of dishonesty, betrayal—and sincere admiration.

With his extended family of about forty-five individuals, Abd el-Kader first traveled by sea from Djemaa Ghazaouet to the port of Oran. Arriving on December 25, 1847, the Emir was greeted by a small crowd of loyal but sad Arabs, and a welcome surprise. Father Suchet, the courageous priest who had helped carry out the prisoner exchange back in 1841, had come to convey gratitude from Bishop Dupuch for Abd el-Kader's decision to stop fighting. It was not the last time the Emir would hear from Dupuch.

From Oran, the Emir and his group crossed the Mediterranean to the port city of Toulon on the southern coast of France. Now they had to face a much longer voyage to the eastern end of the Mediterranean. They were told that negotiations were under way in both Egypt and Constantinople to arrange for the Emir's exile. That sounded reasonable.

But something seemed wrong. Shouldn't there have been signs of preparations for a long sea voyage? Abd el-Kader saw nothing of the sort.

In fact, the next thing he and his people knew, they were being locked up in a quarantine station, as though for some infectious disease. Ten days passed. Then the Emir and his family were taken to a grim, prison-like fortress near the harbor, Fort Lamalgue. The rest of the Algerians were taken to another fort.

What had become of General Lamoricière's promise, confirmed by the royal prince himself? It was on the basis of that promise, after all, that Abd el-Kader had agreed to end resistance. Now the French government—for no apparent reason—seemed reluctant to live up to its commitment.

Abd el-Kader began to protest, forcefully and eloquently. Deprived of his freedom and the open spaces and beauty of his homeland, now he was being denied what had firmly been guaranteed him. Unendurable! He also stressed the matter of French honor, insisting that France live up to the ideals of its high civilization. Surely, he argued, the government understood that it was in France's own interest to behave honestly, to protect its reputation among the European powers? The Emir argued from every angle. Dignified and proper he might be, in keeping with his natural character and training as a marabout, but he would not suffer in silence.

Still he received no answers or assurances. So, like a field commander who must adjust to the terrain and the enemy's tactics, the Emir realized he would have to make some changes himself. He was responsible, after all, for his people.

Knowing the importance of discipline for keeping up morale, Abd el-Kader established a daily routine of prayer, reading, writing, and visiting. Observers were impressed by the way the captives, who kept strictly to themselves, followed their routine religiously. It was almost as though the French fort had become a sort of Islamic monastery, like the *zawiya* where Abd el-Kader had been educated in his youth. The daily pattern of life provided some degree of comfort for the Algerians—except for the many French soldiers guarding them at all times.

Meanwhile, Abd el-Kader kept on asking why the French government was not living up to its promise. All he got was vague, evasive answers.

The truth was that on the question of what to do with the Emir, the French government was sharply torn. As the satirical press observed, formerly no one knew where to find the Emir—and now no one knew where to put him. On the one hand, General Lamoricière and others argued passionately that promises must be kept. Honor and human decency demanded it—and Great Britain would be only too ready to accuse France of treacherousness if the agreement were broken. The Duke of Aumale emphasized the sincerity and remarkable character of the Emir.

On the other hand, many people believed that Abd el-Kader was still the enemy and would still be dangerous, given any opportunity. They were shocked at the promises made to him. Even the royal family was in conflict, angry that the Duke of Aumale had agreed to those promises. The powerful minister of war insisted that Abd el-Kader—still described as little better than a brutal savage—would be a real danger if turned loose in the Arab world. He would stir up all kinds of trouble; he might even try to return to Algeria and resume fighting. At the very least he would become an inspiration for popular uprisings among the Arab subjects of the Ottoman Empire. Far better to keep him locked up!

And there was another critical issue. No one had forgotten about the slaughter of the French prisoners-of-war at Abd el-Kader's camp in the spring of 1846. Stirred up by the popular press, many people still believed that Abd el-Kader himself was to blame. More and more, public opinion and the popular press were a force to be reckoned with in French politics.

A FRIEND AND A NEW PROPOSAL

Meanwhile, at the gloomy fort, Abd el-Kader at least had a sympathetic listener. A capable translator was assigned to him, Lieutenant General Eugène Daumas, whom the Emir had known and respected during the early years of his fight against the French. Daumas, reluctantly, played a complex role. He had to interpret French actions to Abd el-Kader, report secretly on Abd el-Kader's words and moods, and win his confidence enough to persuade him to respond as the government wished him to. Abd el-Kader undoubtedly realized all of that, yet a strong friendship grew between the two men. Daumas did what he could to make the Algerians' lot a little easier.

In mid-January, Abd el-Kader had a small victory. Thanks to his continuing protests, those of his followers who had been sent to other places of imprisonment were brought to Fort Lamalgue. No matter how crowded and uncomfortable the conditions at the fort, the Algerians wanted to be together.

But what about the French government's most important promise to the Emir? One day in late winter, Daumas was instructed to present, as persuasively as possible, a new proposal from the minister of war. The Algerians had two choices. They could indeed go to Alexandria, Egypt, if they insisted. But they would have to live under constant guard for the indefinite future. Alternatively—and so much better!—they could all stay in France. There they would live in a country chateau with beautiful surroundings, privacy, and all the horses they wanted. In this way they would release the government from the promise made back at the "pirates' base."

Abd el-Kader was shocked by the government's behavior, but he had no trouble deciding between the two alternatives. He would choose life in Egypt, even under house arrest. Life in France, where the people and customs were so unfamiliar to the Algerians, would never be suitable for him and his people. It would be a death sentence. As for the temptations of luxury, he told Daumas: "If you placed in my burnoose [hooded cloak] all the diamonds and treasure of the world, I would throw them without hesitation into the sea in front of us."[1] No, nothing could distract him from what had first been promised.

Daumas, who kept a careful record of his conversations with the Emir, realized he would get nowhere trying to promote the government's offer. Abd el-Kader's mood swung between anger, desperate unhappiness, and resignation. As he told Daumas during bad moments, he might appear to be alive, but he was really only a dead man. Finally Daumas suggested that Abd el-Kader write directly to King Louis-Philippe, asking for justice and a personal meeting with the king. Abd el-Kader wrote an eloquent letter, asserting that it was the Almighty's will that he put himself, "as a child," in the king's hands.

While Abd el-Kader waited for an answer, Daumas tried to provide a little variety in the lives of the Algerians. One day he took Abd el-Kader and some of his men to visit the naval arsenal in Toulon, reporting afterward that the Algerians were well received wherever they went. But Abd el-Kader refused any further excursions. He did not want to give the impression of accepting, let alone enjoying, his life in France. He was a *prisoner*, not a "guest." And he did not like being stared at in the street.

Much more to Abd el-Kader's liking were his conversations with Daumas and others. Increasing numbers of French visitors were already coming to see him. Remembering the surprisingly warm relationship he had found with the bishop and priest in Algiers, Abd el-Kader took a particular interest in discussing religion. He also wanted to talk with Daumas and others about philosophy, France and its baffling politics, and all sorts of military matters. He asserted his own views tactfully but firmly. When Daumas asked what advice he might have for the new rulers of Algeria, he replied, "Do as I did. Govern only with the Law in your hand, and then you will succeed."[2]

Although devoutly committed to the teachings of Islam, Abd el-Kader also knew when to be flexible in his behavior. When Daumas invited the Emir to have dinner with him and his wife, Abd el-Kader agreed—even though eating in the company of another man's wife, not related by family ties, would have been unacceptable in Algerian society at that time. He found Madame Daumas, stylishly but modestly dressed, intelligent and charming.

On another day, in late February, Abd el-Kader agreed to have his portrait painted. Many traditional Muslim societies prohibited depicting human likenesses, but Abd el-Kader saw no need for such rigidity. Soon a well-known artist arrived in the Emir's quarters in the gloomy fort. But the artist had come for more than one purpose. Along with his brushes and oil paints, he brought a secret message from the king.

Louis-Philippe had at last responded to Abd el-Kader's eloquent letter. Yes, he would honor the promise made to the Emir. The Algerians would be set free.

REVOLUTION AGAIN

The Algerians' rejoicing did not last long. Just a few days later, France went into another political tailspin. The year 1848 was a time of political turmoil in much of Europe, and in France, King Louis-Philippe was brought down by the Paris mob. On February 28th he gave up the throne and fled to England. The monarchy was finished, and a new republic was declared. What would this mean for Abd el-Kader's hopes?

The Emir could not understand how it was possible for the great French "sultan," as he had referred to the king, suddenly to vanish. Nor could he make sense of a government run by committee. How could five heads, instead of one supreme and wise head like the chief of a tribe, make decisions?

A high official of the new republic soon came from Paris to meet the famous prisoner. Abd el-Kader reminded Émile Ollivier that he had never been overcome by force of arms, and that he had voluntarily promised never to return to or interfere in Algeria. Ollivier reported to his government that Abd el-Kader's oath, "which is known throughout the length and breadth of Algeria, makes it impossible for him to attempt a *coup*, because he would thereby lose that reputation for integrity which has been his whole strength."[3] Ollivier's efforts, however, did not get far. The leaders of the Second Republic did not consider themselves bound by promises made by kings or princes. No decision could be made on Abd el-Kader's future until elections were held and the government had a chance to settle down.

The new government, just like the one it had replaced, was split by conflicting views. Many people, including such well-known writers as Victor Hugo and Alexis de Tocqueville, weighed in on the subject of Algeria. Some said France should keep only the port cities and let the native chieftains run the rest of the country, as under the Turks. Others said that France must not neglect its noble *mission civilisatrice*— "civilizing mission"—in North Africa. Still others, asserting that hatred was inevitable between European settlers and the native people, insisted that France must quickly strengthen the colonial society and make it dominant.

Finally the Second Republic decided *not* to honor the promises made to Abd el-Kader. When he received this bad news from the unhappy Daumas, the Emir burst out, "I am betrayed—and by those in whom I had placed my trust. If you keep us here, many of us will take our lives."[4] His people, he feared, would lose faith in him, and it was no small matter for the head of a tribe to lose the confidence of his people.

In April 1848, three of Abd el-Kader's brothers and their families—some thirty-five people in total—arrived from Algiers. They had expected to go with the Emir to the promised new home in the east, but instead they found themselves prisoners. Abd el-Kader poured out his grief to Daumas. "I am a prisoner in defiance of international law, and now my family, which was free, is lured into an insidious trap. I never would have believed that a nation such as yours could sink so low as to snare men the way children cruelly snare little birds."[5]

So strongly did Abd el-Kader complain about betrayal that some government officials thought he might try to escape—or else the British might attempt a dramatic rescue. Abd el-Kader could not remain on the Mediterranean coast: it was too accessible. The Algerians would have to be moved from Toulon, away from the sea. And so it was decided. Abd el-Kader would be sent to a chateau near the Pyrenees, the mountain range between France and Spain.

A MOVE TO A BETTER PRISON

The French government tried to make the move sound attractive. After all, the chateau at Pau held a special place in French history and hearts. It was the birthplace of an important French king, Henry IV, who had tried to unite his country when it was torn by religious wars between Catholics and Protestants in the sixteenth century. Pau was in a beautifully scenic area, with a delightful climate. Everything would be far more agreeable than at Fort Lamalgue, Abd el-Kader was assured, and he would really be just a "temporary guest."

The Emir knew very well, however, that the chateau would still be a prison. Worse, only his family and servants would stay with him at the chateau. The rest of the Algerians would be held elsewhere as political prisoners. Once more Abd el-Kader exploded in despair and fury. "Drag us through the streets, over stones, through brambles, till our bodies are in shreds! We will be an example to the whole world that all people everywhere may know what lies in store for those who trust you in the future!"[6] In a calmer vein, the Emir emphasized that it was not "blood" that was important but loyalty and friendship; his people had sacrificed everything to stay with him. And at last the government relented. A total of seventy-seven Algerians were counted as "immediate family."

On April 23, the Algerians set out for their next place of captivity, by ship, canal boat, and finally by coach over the foothills of the Pyrenees. What sort of a welcome did they find in the town of Pau?

Engraving of Abd el-Kader in
combat during the 1840s

Desert horsemen, mid-19th century

Camel caravan at the El-Kantara Oasis, Algeria

Kabylie Mountain Road, Algeria

Portrait of Marshal Thomas-Robert
Bugeaud, depicted as
Govener-General of Algeria,
by Charles-Philippe Larivière

Engraving of General
August Lamoricière

The Chateau of Amboise, where Abd el-Kader was held captive

Painting of Louis-Napoleon announcing the liberation of Abd el-Kader
on October 16, 1852, by Ange Tissier, 1861. Abd el-Kader's mother, Lalla Zohra,
kisses the hand of Louis-Napoleon.

Portrait of Emperor Napoleon III, by Alexandre Cabanel, c. 1865

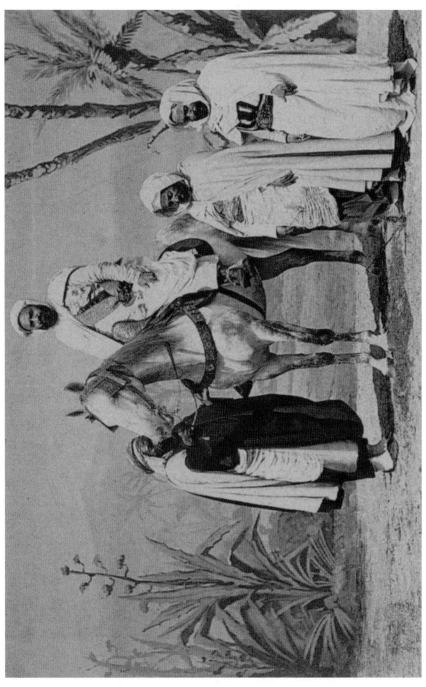

Abd el-Kader with his most faithful companions,
photo by Louis-Jean Delton, 1865

Photo of Abd el-Kader at his home in Damascus, attributed to
Gustave Le Gray, c. 1860

A Damascus street, photo by Félix Bonfils, c. 1860

Painting of Abd el-Kader protecting the Christian community of Damascus during the riots of 1860, by Jean-Baptiste Huysmans, 1861

The destruction of the Christian quarter of Damascus, photo by Francis Bedford, 1862

Abd el-Kader, photo by Étienne Carjat, 1865

CHAPTER 9

THE IMPRISONED CELEBRITY

Many of the citizens of Pau were appalled at the thought of the Emir living among them. The local press called him the "monster of the desert." Some people argued that it was an insult for their famous and recently restored chateau to be inhabited by "a horde of savages who would be happy to wreck it." The tapestries and antique furnishings were carefully put away before the Algerians moved in.

Abd el-Kader was not any happier than the people of Pau. The glorious view of the mountains could be seen only from windows in which iron bars had just been set, and soldiers stood at every strategic spot in the chateau. The French government clearly did not regard the Algerians as "guests." Moreover, the trusted Daumas was no longer with Abd el-Kader, and the two men both regretted the change. The next translator assigned to the job, fortunately, was also well qualified. Estève Boissonnet was a kind and sympathetic man and the author of scholarly works on Algeria.

THE COMPASSIONATE WARRIOR

ABD EL-KADER AT THE CHATEAU OF PAU

The mayor of Pau made a courtesy call on May 3rd, as the chateau's new residents were still getting settled. He evidently brought back an encouraging report, for members of the local society began to steel their nerves and make visits to meet the Emir. It helped, indeed, that nineteenth-century Europeans were fascinated by the exotic, romantic Orient. As fears and prejudices faded, the people of Pau began to find the newcomers intriguing. In fact, they realized, they had the most famous Arab of the time in their midst! The dignified Emir became an object of great interest. Even if somewhat melancholy in manner, he could turn on the charm and wit, especially with ladies, and his courtesy and refinement made an impression on everyone.

The waves of visitors grew larger and bolder. People started coming from all over France. Abd el-Kader finally had to limit his visiting hours to just two days a week, so he could have time for the reading, prayer, and reflection that were such an important part of his life.

Occasionally a visitor had a special reason for wanting to pay respects. A man whose father had served under Napoleon Bonaparte presented Abd el-Kader with a ring containing a bit of stone from Napoleon's tomb. The more Abd el-Kader learned about Napoleon, the more interested he became, admiring both Napoleon's military brilliance and his moral courage in adversity. There were striking similarities, Abd el-Kader noted, between the objectives, strategies, and fates of the two leaders. With other military visitors, men he might formerly have tried to defeat with every means possible, Abd el-Kader was also polite and correct. He could even enjoy the irony of his situation. "After all," he said to one group, "many officers in the French army are indebted to me. Without me, many of your colonels would still be captains and your generals still colonels."[1]

CHAPTER 9: THE IMPRISONED CELEBRITY

One special visitor lightened the Emir's days: Monsignor Dupuch, formerly the Bishop of Algiers. When the Christian cleric and the Muslim marabout finally did meet in person, it was as though they were lifelong friends.

Many observers found a certain trait in the Emir's behavior remarkable—and it would be considered just as striking today. It was his "forgiveness of enemies." To be sure, the Emir did at times have outbursts of anger when the betrayal seemed especially cruel, and he did say harsh words against the French government, using surprisingly vivid language. But those moments seem to have become increasingly rare as the months passed and he accepted the reality of his imprisonment. Then, gradually, the Emir's special form of forgiveness became evident. On many occasions he expressed admiration for French military prowess, ideals of human rights, and civilization. He even suggested possible reasons that might explain the government's decisions against him.

Daumas, on learning of Dupuch's proposed visit, wrote to him about the Emir. "You will find him gentle, simple, affectionate, modest, resigned, never complaining; excusing his enemies—even those at whose hands he may yet have much to suffer—and never allowing evil to be spoken of them in his presence."[2]

ABD EL-KADER'S FAMILY

Although the Algerians kept to themselves in the chateau, they entered the cultural life of Pau on a couple of occasions. Abd el-Kader attended a piano concert and particularly enjoyed the pieces by Schubert; he would have liked them to be longer, he said. And when a circus came to town, he allowed his brother to take some of the children.

From the onset of his captivity, Abd el-Kader had taken on the role of "father," responsible not only for his own family and servants but for the welfare of each and every one of his followers. "We are one family," he told his captors repeatedly. One bitter February day while they were still inside the bone-chilling stone walls of the fortress at Toulon, Daumas had found Abd el-Kader with no wood for a fire. He suggested getting some from the Emir's companions, but Abd el-Kader responded, "No." If it were in his power, he would have given *them* more. He went on to say that if he were like typical "great chiefs" who only *took* from their people, "would the Arabs have continued to fight as they did? Would they have sacrificed everything—their fortunes, flocks, lives—to follow me?"[3]

But as the months dragged on, Abd el-Kader's sense of responsibility grew ever heavier and the thought that he had unwittingly led all these people into captivity tormented him. So many people were suffering because of him! Cold, illness, fear, forced idleness—because of him! Yet he had to keep their spirits up. When he received the bad news that the government definitely regarded him as a prisoner, he kept it to himself and went on reassuring his people.

Inevitably, however, the months of captivity and seclusion were taking a toll on all the Algerians' health. Several died, including three of the Emir's young children. They were buried in a small plot on the grounds of the chateau. During August, when the Muslims observed the month of fasting called Ramadan, the women and children grew seriously weakened. They refused French male doctors but accepted visits by nurses from a local convent, the Dominican Sisters of Charity. Abd el-Kader was deeply grateful for the kindness and healing ways of the nuns.

FLICKERING HOPES, NEW MOVES

At one point, sudden changes in Paris seemed to turn everything around. In June of 1848, France was once again caught up in revolutionary fever. When the blood was washed from the streets and the political dust had settled, there seemed reason for hope. General Lamoricière, who had made the original promise to the Emir, was now minister of war, and Abd el-Kader promptly wrote to him. But for whatever reasons, no response came from Paris.

Weeks passed, and hopes faded. Some of the Algerian men became so unhappy they thought up a drastic scheme. They would simply throw themselves, unarmed, against their guards, which would almost certainly result in their deaths. Abd el-Kader quickly put an end to the plan, although he could certainly understand their desperation. Learning of this incident, Lamoricière knew what a scandal it would have been for the government if successful. He promptly ordered that all the prisoners should be released—except for Abd el-Kader. The Emir's men refused. They would stay together, no matter what.

In Paris, meanwhile, the French government was alarmed by the Algerians' threat of group suicide and their insistence on staying with their commander. Now the ministers argued that the Emir was too close to Spain. The British might be tempted to help him escape over the mountains. Yes, the Algerians would have to be moved again. This time, however, they must be kept someplace close to Paris, where they could be more carefully guarded.

So Abd el-Kader and his large family prepared to move once more. Their arrival in Pau, in late April of 1848, had been greeted with hostility, but their departure in early November was totally different. In just a few months the townspeople, Catholic nuns and clerics, and many others had been won over by the Emir's gracious behavior. Abd el-Kader now felt himself in friendly surroundings. As an expression of appreciation, he let his translator Boissonnet take him on a brief tour of the chateau and its treasures—the tapestries, furniture, art, and precious objects that had been carefully put away before the arrival of the "savages."

THE COMPASSIONATE WARRIOR

When it was time to leave, Abd el-Kader requested that he be driven in an open carriage through the streets to say farewell to the people of Pau. The journey of the Algerians northward to Paris was like a royal procession. In the large city of Bordeaux, Monsignor Dupuch arranged a warm welcome. All along the way, Abd el-Kader was greeted by dignitaries, enthusiastic crowds, and in the town of Nantes, a thirteen-cannon military salute.

ABD EL-KADER AT AMBOISE

The prisoners' destination was another famous castle, the Chateau of Amboise. It rose on a cliff high over the Loire, a major river of France, and in the sixteenth century had been a favorite residence of French kings. It had a dark history as well, having witnessed gruesome executions of hundreds of prisoners during the religious wars later in that century. By the 1800s the chateau was in poor shape—Napoleon Bonaparte had even used it as a prison. As restorations were under way, it was in a livable condition when it became the next residence of the Emir Abd el-Kader.

Still, it was a prison, and now heavier restrictions were imposed. For a while the French government seemed obsessed with security. No visitors without special permission. No letter-writing unless authorized—which must have been a hardship for a man who expressed himself in writing so frequently and fluently. Two hundred soldiers were now assigned to guard the Algerians.

For months Abd el-Kader kept to his rooms, refusing even to walk outdoors in the fresh air. Only the air of freedom could make him well again, he said. At least this chateau had more light and no bars on the windows. But how long would the Algerians have to live there? No answers, not a hint. In a mood of resignation, they went on with their daily routine of prayer, meditation, visiting among themselves, and educating their children. They had no way of knowing how very slowly the wheels of justice were turning—or even whether those wheels were turning at all.

MORE POLITICAL SURPRISES

Then, once again French politics went through a sudden, unexpected turnover. The long-awaited elections to create an official Second Republic were held in December 1848. Abd el-Kader was actually a write-in candidate for president, thanks to enthusiastic friends in Bordeaux. That, of course, was simply a gesture of admiration—but the real winner was just as improbable. It was the candidate considered *least* likely to win: Louis-Napoleon, nephew of the great Napoleon Bonaparte.

Many people thought Louis-Napoleon was an impractical man, too much of a dreamer, an unrealistic fighter for lost causes. Like his famous uncle he had grandly ambitious ideas for his country's foreign adventures, but not the skill to make them succeed. At the same time, he was genuinely an idealist, concerned about helping oppressed peoples. When Abd el-Kader learned that the new president had sympathetic views regarding the people of Algeria, his hopes rose again.

Louis-Napoleon listened to the Emir's supporters. But he listened more carefully to his own ministers and members of the French parliament, who insisted on keeping Abd el-Kader a prisoner. They argued that conditions in Algeria were still unsettled and dangerous. The native people chafed under military rule, and the French army was much reduced. Many European colonists were returning home, discouraged by the hard life in Algeria. And no one could keep the job of governor-general for more than a few weeks. No, this was certainly not the time to set the Emir Abd el-Kader free. How could he be trusted not to return to Algeria and cause even more trouble?

THE COMPASSIONATE WARRIOR

Besides, there was the matter of that dreadful massacre of the French prisoners-of-war. Members of the government, referring to the North Africans' earlier unsavory reputation as pirates, still claimed that Abd el-Kader was to blame. The sensationalist press whipped up public outrage. So, let the Emir go on ranting about broken promises and his liberty—but keep him locked up! Louis-Napoleon decided not to make any decisions that might rattle his still shaky presidency.

SUPPORT FROM MANY DIRECTIONS

On the other hand, a number of influential people in the government did speak for the Emir. Military leaders, too, spoke up. The Emir's old adversary, the Marshall Bugeaud, now tried to be helpful, in his way. He wrote to the Emir "as a true friend" and urged that the Algerians agree to settle happily in the countryside of France, where they could enjoy a healthy life "cultivating the soil."

In the early spring of 1849, Monsignor Dupuch succeeded—with much difficulty—in visiting Abd el-Kader at Amboise. A few months later he published a booklet; it was to set the record straight about the Emir, he said. Focusing on the accusation about the prisoners-of-war, Dupuch tried to demonstrate that Abd el-Kader's sincerity and humane character completely refuted such a charge. As evidence he discussed the Emir's efforts to end barbaric traditions in warfare, his concern for *all* prisoners-of-war, and the many former prisoners who had written to and visited the Emir to thank him for the kind treatment they had received.

Dupuch also told how, when war started again in 1839, Abd el-Kader had fully paid the European advisers hired to help with his army and munitions industries, even though they had not been able to finish their work. He had heard this from their own mouths, Dupuch added, concluding that all this testimony was powerful proof of the Emir's humane character.

CHAPTER 9: THE IMPRISONED CELEBRITY

Meanwhile, Abd el-Kader was not forgotten by the wider world. In fact, his fame grew steadily. Numerous articles and books were published about him in France, almost as though everyone who had ever been to Algeria wanted to write a book about the Emir.

In Great Britain, too, people were fascinated by his story; and if that story reflected badly on France, so much the better. The British public happily made a popular hero of Abd el-Kader. At the race tracks against huge odds, a small horse named Abd el-Kader won the Grand National Steeple Chase in both 1850 and 1851!

Journalists and poets alike took up their pens on behalf of this hero, who now appeared incredibly romantic. While the British press had earlier enjoyed reporting the hard time that Abd el-Kader was giving the French in war, now the tributes expressed sympathy with the betrayed Emir. The famous English poet William Makepeace Thackeray published a poem about Abd el-Kader imprisoned in Toulon, which began:

> No more, thou lithe and long-winged hawk, of desert-life
> for thee;
> No more across the sultry sands shalt thou go swooping
> free:
> Blunt idle talons, idle-beak, with spurning of thy chain,
> Shatter against thy cage the wing thou ne'er may'st spread
> again.[4]

A member of the English aristocracy wrote a stirring poem that ended—

> God save Abd-el-Kader! Tho' banish'd he be,
> Tho' the Frank rule the plain, and the Frank keep the sea;
> For the tribes of El Gharb, from Biskara to Rif,
> Shall arise at the neigh of thy war horse—Great Chief![5]

And from the pen of "an English Lady" came this tribute:

> The aged Emir bows to fate: His sorrows claim a peaceful
> grave;
> He seeks no ransom from the State, save this, which valor
> grants the brave.[6]

Another English aristocrat, the Marquis of Londonderry, decided to see what he could do in person. With his wife and daughter he set out to visit Abd el-Kader in the chateau at Amboise. Permission was granted—but the French authorities decided to make the experience as unpleasant as possible for the interfering English. They were kept waiting for several hours in one chilly, cluttered room after another, until finally they were allowed to see the prisoner. Abd el-Kader welcomed the visitors with warmth, and later said farewell with such a firm embrace that Londonderry complained of a sore neck afterwards. Nonetheless he wrote, "I think this indescribably interesting and noble old chief was much pleased and greatly affected by our visit."[7] (In his mid-forties and still very fit, Abd el-Kader was hardly old—but the English loved that sort of image.)

Londonderry wrote to Louis-Napoleon, urging that even if there were some slight risk in setting Abd el-Kader free, it would be greatly offset by the world's admiration of French generosity. Louis-Napoleon answered with great care: "I shall be very glad to see the Emir, but I can only see him to announce good news."[8] Disappointed but determined to continue his efforts, the Marquis and his family went back to London.

RESIGNATION—AND LOOSER BINDS

As the months of captivity became years, the fire of Abd el-Kader's protest dimmed and he seemed to grow more resigned to his fate. He would simply wait, trusting, for the new president to set him free. He told visitors that he thought France should not be judged on just a moment in time, but over its long history.

Abd el-Kader's five-year imprisonment was not, in fact, time *out* of his life. He did not retreat into discouragement and lethargy, intellectual or spiritual. On the contrary, he kept growing. Having determined to learn about French thinking and customs, he developed a much more accurate—and for the most part, positive—understanding of his former enemies. The flood of visitors gave him opportunity to observe and reflect on all sorts of European people and their mentalities. His captors were wise to allow this free interchange.

The more Abd el-Kader learned and thought about French civilization—and western civilization in general—the more his interest grew. He saw the strengths, and the weaknesses and failings. He even tried to envisage a role for himself that might help strengthen the spiritual life of the nation that held him captive. With the encouragement of his trusted interpreter Boissonnet, he set down in writing his thoughts about religion, politics, science, history, and culture. The "Letter to the French" that eventually emerged will be described later in the story.

At the same time, Abd el-Kader had leisure to reflect more on his own culture and to assess the "broader picture"—his own tradition and its values side-by-side with the civilization of the west. At one point the Emir's former interpreter Eugène Daumas, who was writing a book about the Sahara, wanted the expert help that only Abd el-Kader could provide. In the part about "Horses of the Sahara," Abd el-Kader wrote detailed commentaries about Arabian horses, a treasury of information and opinion from one who really knew his horses. In the second part, about human life in the desert, he contributed a chapter about the importance of hunting among the tribes—possibly the definitive discussion of how hyenas, lions, and leopards hunt, and are hunted in turn (or were in those days). This book, co-authored with Daumas, must have been like a brisk ride in the desert breezes for Abd el-Kader.

Gradually, even while heated debates went on in the French Chamber of Deputies, the government relaxed the restrictions placed on Abd el-Kader and his people. In 1850, as a test, Louis-Napoleon allowed nineteen Algerians to return to their country, and there was no uproar from press or public. A complimentary poem that Abd el-Kader wrote to the president led to a careful correspondence between the two men.

The Emir also began to allow himself a little more freedom. He took walks in the formal gardens of the chateau, and he learned to play chess, admiring the game for its mental discipline and similarity to military strategy. In the spring of 1851 he started to accept a few social invitations, returning the good will shown him by citizens of Amboise, and he visited other chateaus in the region. He allowed some of the male Algerians to explore the town of Amboise on their own. The days when Abd el-Kader rejected all things French were behind him. Now he grasped opportunities that would lead to new learning and experience.

But for many of the imprisoned Algerians, cut off so long from their normal way of life, depression was never far away, nor were illness and death. In addition to those who had succumbed at Pau, twenty-five adults and children were resting in a small cemetery in the chateau gardens at Amboise by the summer of 1852. Some were members of the Emir's immediate family. As he walked among the gravestones, he must have reflected sadly that he still could do nothing except wait . . . with faith that eventually justice would be done.

CHAPTER 10

FREEDOM AND A NEW LIFE IN EXILE

On an afternoon in mid-October of 1852, nearly five years after he had given up his fight against the French, Abd el-Kader was strolling outdoors when he received an unexpected order. He was to appear immediately in one of the chateau's formal salons. There he found Louis-Napoleon, President of the Republic, waiting for him.

"Abd el-Kader," announced Louis-Napoleon, "I have come to tell you that you are set at liberty." Then the interpreter Boissonnet, with much emotion, translated the President's written statement. "For a long time, as you know, your captivity has caused me genuine grief, for it reminded me constantly that the government which preceded me had not kept its promises to an unhappy enemy. . . ."[1]

Abd el-Kader had already recognized one vital word—*liberté*, freedom. His long wait was now nearly over. Kneeling, he kissed the hand of the president.

In the ceremonies that immediately followed, the Emir's mother Lalla Zohra was presented to Louis-Napoleon. Then the president and the Algerians sat down together to a dinner of couscous, the traditional

North African wheat dish, served with vegetables and meat. In his gratitude Abd el-Kader is reported to have said, "Others have overthrown me and imprisoned me, but only Louis-Napoleon has conquered me."[2]

ABD EL-KADER'S LIBERATION: HOW IT HAPPENED

What brought about this sudden change in Abd el-Kader's fate? The first answer is that an interesting assortment of friends and supporters—Monsignor Dupuch, Lord Londonderry, Marshall Bugeaud and numerous others—had been working behind the scene for years, trying to persuade both the government and the French public that it was not only honorable but safe for the Emir to be liberated. The efforts of so many individuals, with widely differing backgrounds and concerns, were proof of the Emir's remarkable ability to inspire loyalty and determination to work for justice.

There were other influences as well, and one was the character of Louis-Napoleon himself. In his own political career he had known imprisonment and discouragement, which helped him to sympathize with the Emir and the Algerian people. Another factor was the way Abd el-Kader's fate so often hung upon the turbulence of the French political scene. During the sixty years up until 1852, the French people had lived under a monarchy, a revolutionary mob and its leaders, a republic, an empire under Napoleon Bonaparte, another monarchy, another republic, and then a republic ruled by a popularly elected president—who had just seized more power and added "prince" to his title.

And now Prince-President Louis-Napoleon wanted to be *emperor*! In the month just before his decision to release Abd el-Kader, he had been touring France to test public opinion. He was pleased to find that people were fed up with the instability of government "by committee." They were ready to relinquish some of the freedoms and rights of a democratic form of government for a firm hand at the helm. And they were very eager indeed for a revival of national glory. In short, the French wanted to be an empire again under the rule of one man—especially a man from the family of their national hero, Napoleon Bonaparte.

Reassured of his popularity, Louis-Napoleon felt the time was right to carry out his country's promises. It would be safe to set Abd el-Kader free.

THE LION IN PARIS

Before leaving France, Abd el-Kader wanted to see Paris, learn more about French civilization, and express his appreciation for the support shown him by so many French people. On October 28, 1852, he set off for a red-carpet tour of the French capital.

He arrived to find all Paris rejoicing over the prospect of dramatic political change. Invited to the famed Paris opera that very evening, Abd el-Kader accepted when assured that Louis-Napoleon would be attending. It turned out to be an absolutely thrilling evening at the opera. The audience went wild when a musical piece was presented celebrating the new empire-to-come. "Empire is peace!" sang the performers. Louis-Napoleon invited Abd el-Kader to the royal box, where the two men greeted each other warmly for all to see.

The next day, at his request, Abd el-Kader's tour started with some of the great churches of Paris. First on the itinerary was a huge monument resembling a Roman temple. The Madeleine had been built by Napoleon Bonaparte in honor of his army, but later turned into a Roman Catholic church. Standing beside the priest, Abd el-Kader prayed silently at the altar. The watching crowds were amazed, and Abd el-Kader is said to have been pleased that they could witness a Muslim worshipping in a Christian church. Then to the famous medieval cathedral of Notre Dame, where Abd el-Kader took interest in both the religious items and the robes that the first Napoleon had worn for his coronation as emperor in 1804.

And then to the National Artillery Museum, the Hippodrome to watch an aerial battle between two balloonists, the National Library, a hospital for war veterans, the tomb of Napoleon Bonaparte, theatrical performances and more opera, and the horse races. At the National Printing Works the Emir commented, "Yesterday I saw cannons with which ramparts are toppled. Today I saw the machine with which kings are toppled."[3] From his own experience he knew about the power of the press, for both good and ill.

Whenever he was allowed a little time at his hotel, all sorts of visitors poured in—more than three hundred in all. As usual Abd el-Kader, who always seemed able to think of the right thing to say to each individual, spoke graciously to women as well as men, to the modest as well as the powerful, scholars as well as society figures, common soldiers as well as generals. His old friend the former bishop of Algiers, Dupuch, arrived one morning in time for breakfast. The Emir was delighted, reminding his visitor that he, Dupuch, had been the first Frenchman to believe in him.

In the midst of all the acclaim and mutual admiration, the suspicions regarding the massacre of French prisoners in 1846 seemed to have faded away. But for a few people they lingered. One of the officers who had been spared when the common soldiers were killed, came to see the Emir in Paris and raised the subject. Once more, Abd el-Kader explained that he had neither known about nor approved of the deed. Then why, asked his visitor, did he not punish the culprits?

In a few words Abd el-Kader made clear not only the dire situation he had faced, but his steadfast principles. "I could not do so. My chiefs were in revolt and no longer obeyed me, my soldiers were embittered by defeat and had but a handful of barley to live on. Do not question me further—I do not wish to accuse another."[4] At last the French officer understood.

On Abd el-Kader's final day in Paris he went to the famous palace at Versailles, home of French kings for centuries. On that occasion, seated on the white horse that Louis-Napoleon had given him, he watched the cavalry charges and other military routines performed in his honor. Then came a display of water works—elaborate fountains and jets in the famous formal gardens—and a huge banquet.

By all accounts, Abd el-Kader had taken Paris by storm. He was, as the newspapers said, "the lion of the day."

LAST DAYS IN FRANCE AND DEPARTURE

Indeed, more than a lion: almost a Frenchman. When a popular vote was taken on November 22, 1852, to declare Louis-Napoleon emperor, Abd el-Kader wanted to cast his vote—as a French citizen. Along with thirteen of his Algerian men, he did so. By a curious coincidence, on exactly the same date twenty years earlier, Abd el-Kader had been declared Commander of the Faithful—*against* the French. He made another brief visit to Paris in early December to witness Louis-Napoleon taking his place in history as Emperor Napoleon III.

Back in Amboise, Abd el-Kader got busy writing letters thanking individuals who had helped him, with special gratitude for the nuns of the Dominican Sisters of Charity, who had taken care of the Algerian women and children. One of the sisters described him in this way: "Allowing certain exceptions of a theological nature, there is no Christian virtue that Abd el-Kader does not practice in the highest degree."[5] The townspeople of Amboise raised funds for the care of the small cemetery in the chateau's garden. In turn, Abd el-Kader bought an elegant crystal chandelier from the chateau itself, to present to the parish church.

THE COMPASSIONATE WARRIOR

Finally the Emir and his family and supporters were ready to leave France. Once again their departure was a procession, marked by receptions and crowds along the way, to the busy port of Marseilles on the Mediterranean. There, on December 21, 1852, almost five years to the day after the Emir had stopped fighting, they boarded a large and luxurious ship for the eastern Mediterranean.

But what was Abd el-Kader's destination? Not the Arab cities that he had been promised, Alexandria in Egypt or Acre in Palestine. Instead, once again the French government rearranged the Emir's life. They sent him to the heart of the Ottoman Empire.

The Emir had been informed earlier of this decision. But why the change? Perhaps the emperor, for all his high regard for Abd el-Kader, still worried about allowing him freedom in the Arab countries. In Turkey he could be more closely observed and, if necessary, controlled. Perhaps the French government thought the presence of Abd el-Kader in Turkey could strengthen an alliance with the Ottoman government against Russian encroachments in the Middle East. Possibly, too, the French assumed it wouldn't really make too much difference. One Muslim city, they may have reasoned, was as good as another, and at least the heart of the Ottoman Empire would be more interesting than the provincial towns of Egypt and Palestine.

ABD EL-KADER IN TURKEY

In any case, as Abd el-Kader's ship approached Constantinople, the Turks greeted it properly with a twenty-one-gun salute. Then, after the formalities of welcoming speeches, state dinners, and ceremonial visits, the Algerians were taken to the town of Bursa, a day's journey from Constantinople. By now the Emir's family included more than one hundred people—all his family, he insisted, whether related by blood or marriage, or neither.

CHAPTER 10: FREEDOM AND A NEW LIFE IN EXILE

The residence that awaited them in Bursa was a *khan*, a large building with a spacious open court, the sort of structure used for hundreds of years for the caravans that carried on trade in the eastern world. It was roomy and included baths, but was badly neglected. Fortunately, the French government had decided to provide Abd el-Kader with a generous annual allowance. He was able to fix up the *khan* adequately and also to purchase a more comfortable house in the nearby countryside. There he settled down, using any surplus money to help the local mosques and charities. The town of Bursa, near a mountain range, was scenic and colorful; the fruit was delicious, and the air clean. It was not a bad place to live.

But it had not taken Abd el-Kader long to note a definite coolness on the part of the French diplomats in Constantinople. In France he had been the emperor's friend, welcomed everywhere. Here he still seemed to be regarded with suspicion. His new interpreter, Georges Bullad, a young man from a prominent Syrian Christian family, had grown up in France. Abd el-Kader liked him, but he was aware that Bullad's duties included reading his mail and sending daily reports to the French ministry of war, which still maintained control over his activities. The Emir was no longer a caged hawk, but neither was he able to fly free.

Moreover, the attitude of the Ottoman Turks toward Abd el-Kader—even though they were fellow Muslims—was far from friendly. For a while, some of the Turkish officials worried that he might be politically disruptive and encourage nationalist ideas in the Arab world. For more than three hundred and fifty years the Ottomans had ruled the Arab lands, from what is now Iraq in the east to Algeria in the west. Thanks to their military might they kept order exceedingly well, but beyond that they did very little for the people and tended to consider the Arabs culturally inferior. For his part, Abd el-Kader had not forgotten the Ottoman sultan's indifference to his struggle against the French conquest of his homeland. The fact that the Turkish and Arabic languages are totally different further blocked communication and added to the Algerians' feeling that they did not belong in this new land.

ABD EL-KADER BACK IN PARIS

The Emir endured his exile in Bursa as long as he could. In the summer of 1855 an earthquake badly damaged the town, and it looked to Abd el-Kader like a good time to make a trip back to Paris. He had more than one purpose in mind. Always eager for new knowledge and technology, he wanted to visit the Universal Exposition that was going on in Paris at the time, a huge event with twenty-four thousand exhibitors and five million visitors. He did visit it, again and again, looking closely at the new uses of steam power, modern printing presses, improvements in veterinary science, and not least of all the sewing machines—which reminded him of how he had stitched his own garments by hand as a youth. Modern technology, Abd el-Kader was convinced, was intended by God to serve the common good.

The Emir's main purpose in visiting Paris, however, was to talk frankly—but tactfully—with Napoleon III. He feared that his request might not be received favorably, in view of the emperor's decision to send him to Turkey in the first place.

Again, political conditions played a role in the Emir's fate. France, Britain, and Turkey were at war with Russia in the Crimea, a peninsula that juts into the Black Sea. When he arrived in Paris in September 1855, Abd el-Kader found the French deliriously happy over their victory in one of the major battles. A religious service of thanks was planned at the cathedral of Notre Dame; and after inquiring whether it would please the emperor for him to be there, Abd el-Kader—although ill with cholera—agreed to attend. Weak, supported by a French officer, he was met with loud cheers at the cathedral.

CHAPTER 10: FREEDOM AND A NEW LIFE IN EXILE

Both the Emir and the emperor were high in popularity, which could only help prepare the way for Abd el-Kader's request. When he was able to meet with Napoleon III, he asked whether his place of exile could be changed to an Arab country. He had Damascus in mind, which his translator Georges Bullad had been recommending. When the emperor promptly suggested Damascus, Abd el-Kader just as promptly accepted, and everyone was happy.

Napoleon III provided a steamship to take Abd el-Kader back to Turkey and from there transport him and his family to the port of Beirut. By then the Algerian colony in Bursa had grown to about two hundred individuals, as more and more of his countrymen were choosing to join the Emir in exile. Some had to travel by land to Beirut, where Abd el-Kader arrived on November 24, 1855.

ABD EL-KADER IN SYRIA

The coast of Syria in that area—now the Republic of Lebanon—ran alongside a high and rugged mountain range known as Mount Lebanon. To reach Damascus, a traveler had to cross this mountain range by horse, mule, camel, and foot.

Abd el-Kader set out on his journey with an interesting invitation in hand: to visit the mountain home of a retired British army officer named Colonel Charles Henry Churchill. This adventurous, dynamic, and highly opinionated Englishman had served with a British military expedition to Syria in 1840 and liked Mount Lebanon so much that he decided to stay. He had visited Abd el-Kader in Bursa a couple of years earlier, and the two men had formed an instant friendship.

The route to Colonel Churchill's home passed through an area inhabited mostly by Druze—followers of a religion related to Islam but with differing beliefs and a fiercely independent way of life. As he climbed the mountain road, Abd el-Kader was suddenly met with ferocious gunfire. Fortunately it was the gunfire of welcome, a wildly enthusiastic reception by the Druze chiefs and their men. They knew of his fame, had heard of his coming, and now they begged him to stay—if not for the night, then at least for coffee.

Abd el-Kader was pleased by the warmth of these Druze chiefs—formidable warriors when they needed to be—but he had to push on to Churchill's home, actually an old palace. During their time together, Abd el-Kader and Churchill agreed that the Englishman would later visit the Emir in Damascus for a special project: writing the story of Abd el-Kader's life.

Continuing on his journey, Abd el-Kader and his group descended the slopes of Mount Lebanon, crossed a flat, fertile plain, and ascended another mountain range, lower and less rugged. Finally they reached the valley of the river Barada, where the city of Damascus stood, one of the oldest continually inhabited sites on earth. All along the road the Emir was greeted with cheers of welcome. A group of horsemen rode out to meet him, including friends and former soldiers in his army who had migrated earlier to Syria. Then came throngs of ordinary people and, as he entered the city, a welcome by Turkish troops and military band.

Abd el-Kader had a special reason for wanting to be exiled to Damascus. It was the resting place of his spiritual and intellectual master, the medieval philosopher and mystic Muhyi ad-Din Ibn Arabi, whose works had greatly influenced Abd el-Kader. Ibn Arabi, considered possibly the greatest medieval Sufi thinker, was born in 1165 C.E. in Andalusia, Spain at the height of Islamic civilization. He traveled throughout his life, teaching and writing, and finally settled in Damascus. There he died in 1240 C.E. and was buried in a nearby village called Salihiyya. In his own time, Ibn Arabi had challenged orthodox religious ideas, and had criticized the entrenched religious leaders so much that they took revenge after his death by heaping garbage on his tomb.

The grave had long since been cleaned off and a tomb and shrine erected; but at the time of Abd el-Kader's arrival in Damascus, Salihiyya was considered a shabby and crime-ridden place. Nonetheless, he insisted on visiting the tomb of Ibn Arabi even before entering the city. Salihiyya would play an important role in the Emir's life later on.

IN DAMASCUS, A HOME AT LAST

In Damascus, a pleasant place edged by rocky heights and famous for its fruit trees, Abd el-Kader bought a very large house. It was located in the center of the city, conveniently close to both the Christian quarter of the old city and the Great Mosque, one of the oldest and most impressive in the whole Muslim world.

Actually, Abd el-Kader's house was *three* very large houses joined together, making a structure about as long as a soccer field. Not only was it roomy enough for family and servants, followers and visitors, but it soon became something like a *zawiya*, a religious center open to all. People could come there to converse, seek help, or settle disputes. Every Friday, the Emir gave bread to the poor people of Damascus, who would line up at the house to receive it. Abd el-Kader's huge house was a very wise investment—probably more than even he could have predicted—as events would prove within just a few years.

At last Abd el-Kader was able to step into what he regarded as his true role—a spiritual teacher. His daily classes at the Great Mosque were in constant demand. In particular he taught a group of scholars about the works of his master Ibn Arabi, which helped preserve these important writings for future generations. Abd el-Kader did not think of himself as a spiritual master but as a pilgrim still in search of truth and understanding. He regarded his students not as disciples or followers, but more like fellow seekers.

To be sure, there were pockets of resentment in Damascus. Just as the religious establishment had opposed Ibn Arabi six centuries earlier, the mufti and other Islamic officials of Damascus did not welcome this newcomer, whose superior knowledge and character tended to show up their small-mindedness. But for most of the Muslims of Syria, Abd el-Kader embodied three highly esteemed roles in Islamic culture: a marabout and descendent of the Prophet Muhammad, a scholar and teacher, and not least of all, a defender of Islam and leader of *jihad*.

Yet while he was thankfully returning to the intellectual and spiritual role that he felt God had intended for him, Abd el-Kader was also very much involved in the world around him. He kept up with the news through the Arabic press, and engaged in correspondence and conversation with many people. Moreover, now he could act upon his desire to improve people's lives through modern methods and techniques. He bought tracts of farm land, undertook agricultural projects, promoted road construction, and built a toll bridge. Thanks to the pension that the French government continued to provide, he and his family could live comfortably and at the same time be generous to others.

As a community leader, Abd el-Kader played another important role in the world around him. He had found an Algerian colony already living in Damascus, including former fighters in the struggle against the French conquest. Some men, who had served with France in the Crimean War, came to live in Damascus rather than return to Algeria. Abd el-Kader bought more property, much of it in the center of the city near his large house, and more houses for family members and others in need. The colony grew into a community closely attached to the Emir for his leadership and counsel.

CHAPTER 10: FREEDOM AND A NEW LIFE IN EXILE

These Algerians, and especially the men since they could be active in public life, are often referred to in historical accounts as "Abd el-Kader's Algerians." Their place in the social and political systems of Syria, however, presented something of a problem, and the Turkish overlords had reason to wonder about them. Since they were partially supported by funds from France, did that make them French nationals? Or might they be an arm of imperial France, always reaching for more influence in the area? Or possibly an inspiration for Arab nationalist ideas? At the least they were a symbol of Arab resistance to foreign domination, which could include the Ottoman Empire. Even as Muslims in a predominantly Muslim country, therefore, the Algerians must have felt some of the uneasiness typical of minority status.

At the same time, every so often a brush with officialdom reminded Abd el-Kader that he was still not quite free. When he wanted to make a visit to Jerusalem, Hebron, and Bethlehem, cities that have profound religious significance for Muslims as well as for Jews and Christians, he found roadblocks in his way. Special authorization was needed—not from the Ottomans but from French authorities, who still had their doubts about his loyalty. In 1857 the Emir did succeed in making a short visit to Jerusalem and nearby sites, but only on condition that Georges Bullad should accompany him and report regularly to the French minister of foreign affairs.

Late in 1859 Colonel Churchill, whom Abd el-Kader had visited in Mount Lebanon a few years earlier, came to Damascus. The two men got started on the ambitious but inspiring task of setting down the details of Abd el-Kader's life. Between the Emir's noontime and sundown classes at the Great Mosque, he set aside time every day to talk with Churchill. Their efforts produced one of several nineteenth-century biographies of the Emir, although probably the only one in English.

But as they worked together, could they have had any inkling that a future chapter—perhaps the most dramatic of all—was about to open?

CHAPTER 11

MADNESS IN DAMASCUS

In the spring of 1860, political tensions in Mount Lebanon burst into flame. The heat was soon felt in Damascus, and the Emir Abd el-Kader found himself in the midst of it.

CRISIS IN MOUNT LEBANON

For centuries the people of the mountain had enjoyed a high level of independence. While ruling themselves quite effectively, they were careful to pay their taxes to the Ottoman Empire. For this reason, and the extremely rugged terrain, the Turks had never tried to impose control over the mountain the same way they had over all the surrounding Arab lands. Everything changed, however, in the first half of the nineteenth century. The main causes were social and political developments within Mount Lebanon itself, and the influence of outside powers.

In the northern part of the mountain range lived the Maronite Christians, who followed a form of Roman Catholicism and had long been supported by France. For decades they had been moving south into the part of the mountain populated mostly by the Druze—who were backed by Great Britain, just to keep things more or less balanced. The Maronites, who outnumbered the Druze, were increasing in power, and the Druze felt threatened. The Ottomans saw this growing clash as a chance for them to step in and gain more control.

Under these conditions, violence was probably inevitable. In late May of 1860, many thousands of people were slaughtered, and scores of villages and monasteries destroyed. The Druze were the better fighters, and the Christians suffered the greater losses. Ottoman soldiers, sent supposedly to keep order, joined in against the Christians, killing and looting. Around five thousand Christians, mostly women and children, managed to escape to Damascus. There they were sheltered in Christian homes and churches, inevitably adding to the badly overcrowded conditions in that city. Morale was low and tension high, which gave rise to all sorts of rumors.

ROOTS OF TROUBLE IN DAMASCUS

Although the situation in Damascus was influenced by the trouble in Mount Lebanon, the players and causes were different. The pressure of European interests, both political and economic, had been growing for years. The economy of Syria, and especially Damascus, was affected badly, with local markets and industries forced to give way to European goods. By the middle of the nineteenth century, people were feeling hurt by changes in land ownership, trade, manufacturing, taxation, social developments, and, of course, rising food prices.

The Ottoman administration, which had its own worries, did not help. Its empire, now nearly six hundred years old, was crumbling, and European powers were eagerly waiting for the chance to divide up the remains. With the loss of Greece, Egypt, and Algeria, the Turks tightened their hold on the Arab countries. In this situation the Turkish governor of Damascus, Ahmad Pasha, apparently decided to use the old strategy of "divide and conquer." He could strengthen his support among the Muslims and Druze by turning them against the Christians.

Throughout Syria and Palestine, the Christians were a minority tolerated under Ottoman rule and guaranteed certain rights, so long as they behaved themselves. In the years leading up to 1860 their status had become both more privileged and more endangered, especially because of changes that followed the end of the Crimean War in 1856.

In return for supporting the Ottomans against Russia during the Crimean War, the European powers had imposed certain demands on their ally. Most problematic was the decree that all Christians in the Ottoman Empire should have equal rights with Muslims: civil, political, and military. To many Muslims, the very idea of Christians being officially equal to them was insulting. They hated the new ruling all the more because it was imposed by the interfering and threatening European powers. European support for the Christian communities, many people believed, would open the Arab countries to ever more foreign pressure. In this time of decline, weakness, and confusion in the Muslim world, unscrupulous leaders could easily use the Christians as a scapegoat to blame for all the troubles.

The Christians of Damascus, mostly Greek Orthodox and Greek Catholic, numbered about fifteen thousand out of a total population of around one hundred and sixty thousand. They had naturally welcomed the new reform that gave them equal rights—but some forgot the wise precaution of continuing to behave modestly. In the eyes of many Muslims, they flaunted their new status too boastfully. And there was one matter on which some Christians clearly went too far: they refused to pay their taxes.

Formerly, minorities had been prohibited from serving in the Ottoman army—which was the last thing they wanted to do anyway—and were obliged to pay a tax instead. Under the new rules both Christians and Muslims had to pay a tax to avoid conscription, but the tax on Muslims was much higher. And now some Christians argued that they would no longer pay any tax at all. While the Turks did not really want Christians in the army, they did want the tax money. In 1860, therefore, the Ottoman governor of Damascus decided to make the Christians pay four years' worth of taxes, a heavy burden for many families. Some Christians refused, and their attitude deeply offended many Muslims. It was like a spark in dry grass.

ABD EL-KADER TAKES STEPS

This was the time in his life that Abd el-Kader had intended to devote to peaceful pursuits such as prayer, teaching, and charitable deeds. He might have turned his back on the growing tensions in Damascus: it would not have been unreasonable. Yet he could not escape the world around him, or the role that fate seemed to have cut out for him. Nor did he choose to.

In March 1860, he picked up alarming rumors. It looked like the governor of Damascus, Ahmad Pasha, along with some leaders from the city's Muslims and the Druze villages nearby, were plotting to "correct" the arrogant Christians of Damascus. "Correcting," in that sense, typically included bloodshed.

Fortunately, Abd el-Kader had a strong ally in the French consul, Monsieur Lanusse. He went directly to Lanusse with this information, hoping that the European consuls would confront Ahmad Pasha and persuade him to cancel the plot. Lanusse found the other consuls— from Britain, Russia, Austria, Greece, and Prussia (Germany)—highly skeptical. Nonetheless they designated the Greek consul, who knew Turkish, to talk with the governor. Ahmad Pasha denied the rumors and assured the consuls that there was no cause for concern.

The conspirators laid low for a while. In the meantime, Abd el-Kader instructed his Algerians to be alert and try to stop any talk they heard against the Christians. When Abd el-Kader himself tried to talk with the mufti and other religious leaders, he was rebuffed. Many were envious of this much-admired newcomer and had no interest in cooperating with him.

By early May, aware that Christians were going into hiding or leaving the city, Abd el-Kader was sure that the plot was still alive. Again he went to see Lanusse. Again Lanusse appealed to the other consuls, and this time they all went—although reluctantly—to see Ahmad Pasha. Again the governor denied any problem. He did remark, however, that the Christians were acting rebelliously. He would do what he could, but if there should be a large outbreak of violence, his troops would not be able to control it. The consuls were apparently satisfied with this run-around.

Then came the massacres in Mount Lebanon and the flood of terrified Christian refugees—topped off by wild rumors about Christians planning to attack the Muslims! In June, at Abd el-Kader's urging, Lanusse again talked with the consuls, but this time they simply laughed at his fears.

Now Abd el-Kader took a more active role. He went several times to see Ahmad Pasha, arguing that an attack on the Christians would not only be cowardly but against the laws of both Islam and humanity. The Christians had no arms, no military experience, no way to defend themselves. Abd el-Kader declared, "I will go and put myself with the cavalry in the midst of the Christian quarter, and there I will fight as long as I have breath. I will die, if necessary, for the honor of Islam, whose law forbids crimes of this nature."[1]

The Emir also reached out to the Druze—who had given him such a warm welcome five years earlier but now appeared to be part of the plot. He sent the Druze leaders a firm but careful letter saying, "Some of your horsemen have already been pillaging in the vicinity of Damascus. Such actions are unworthy of a community distinguished for its good sense and sound policy."[2]

At the same time, Abd el-Kader decided to be prepared for trouble. He asked Lanusse to use his special diplomatic privileges to buy all the arms and ammunition he could; the French consul promptly did so and turned them over to the Algerians. The Emir told his men who lived outside Damascus to come into the city, in groups small enough to avoid notice. He urged them to keep trying to persuade people in the city to keep the peace. He talked with every leader he could, from the municipal council of Damascus to village *shaykh*s. Again he tried to reason with the religious leaders, only to get another cold shoulder.

By now the governor, Ahmad Pasha, was growing nervous. The European powers would hold him responsible, Lanusse had warned him, if harm came to the Christians. He moved his family to the citadel, a large fortified area near the center of the city. Then, as he had promised Abd el-Kader, he sent troops to the Christian quarter—but they turned their guns *on* the Christians, rather than the direction from which attacks might come. Some of the Christians tried to appease the soldiers with food and gifts, and others wisely made their escape from Damascus. Finally Ahmad Pasha tried to persuade the Druze leaders outside the city to hold off. But it was too late. All of Damascus was waiting for an incident to light the fuse.

MADNESS ERUPTS

That incident started on Sunday, July 8, 1860, when a few Muslim boys drew crosses on the pavement in the Christian quarter, then spat and scattered trash on them and forced passing Christians to stamp on them. (Accounts vary as to the details.) The Christians complained to the governor, and he—suspiciously ready to cooperate—had the culprits arrested and beaten. The next day the boys were publicly taken to the spot and forced to clean the pavement. An outraged mob quickly formed, ready for action. The whole incident was apparently contrived to look as though Ahmad Pasha was trying to protect the Christians, while actually enraging the Muslims.

And it worked. It touched off one of the most infamous events of modern Middle Eastern history, a week-long nightmare of destruction, looting, and wholesale murder. While Abd el-Kader's role in trying to avert trouble was vital, his actions in the midst of the conflagration made an even more remarkable story.

Knowing that the international representatives would be prime targets of a mob enraged against western influences, Abd el-Kader sent messengers to the consuls who lived or had offices in the Christian quarter, urging them to come immediately to his house. In person he went to the French consulate, which was already surrounded by a mob, and took Lanusse back with him. The British consul, thinking his house safe, stayed until he received a warning; then he got a message delivered to Abd el-Kader, who promptly sent out another rescue mission.

The Russian consulate had already been looted when Abd el-Kader and two of his sons reached it, and the people either murdered or vanished. At the Greek consulate, the Algerians found some three hundred refugees and escorted them all to Abd el-Kader's house. A French doctor with them wrote later, "In those indescribable moments of anguish, heaven, however, sent us a savior! Abd el-Kader appeared, surrounded by his Algerians, around forty of them. He was on horseback and without arms, his handsome figure calm and imposing."[3]

The American vice-consul, Dr. Michael Mishaqa, had a drama of his own. When a mob came to his house, he escaped by the garden, scattering gold coins to distract his pursuers as he ran through the streets. Disguised as a North African, but beaten and bloody, he was finally brought to Abd el-Kader's house and reunited with his family. He recorded his experiences later in a lively history of the area, a book that he entitled *Murder, Mayhem, Pillage, and Plunder.*

RESCUING THE CHRISTIANS

Abd el-Kader had about a thousand of his own men, many of them former fighters, armed and ready. Now they gave top priority to rescuing the Christians.

Horrendous destruction had already swept through the Christian quarter. The Damascus mob—which had started as rabble mostly from the lowest classes—was soon joined by Muslims and Druze from outside the city, crazy with excitement and greedy for the spoils. The rioters first targeted the houses of rich Christians, seizing everything that could be carried away, down to the woodwork and tiles. Before long the whole Christian quarter was burning. Some women and children tried to escape the flames by running across the flat housetops, leaping over spaces between them. Churches, houses, and shops were all looted, and many people murdered.

In the midst of this chaos, Abd el-Kader himself went hurrying through the streets, calling to the Christians to follow him to safety. He described his actions in a letter written on July 18, 1860, which was eventually translated from the Arabic and published by the *New York Times.* "Seeing matters were so desperate," he wrote, "I lost no time in taking under my protection these unfortunate Christians. I sallied forth, taking my Algerians with me, and we were able to save the lives of men, women, and children, and bring them home with us."[4] He also sent groups of his armed men to search through the Christian quarter, shouting, "We are Abd el-Kader's men, don't be afraid! We've come to save you." People emerged from wherever they had tried to find shelter, many filthy from having hidden in drains and wells. A stream of refugees began to find their way to Abd el-Kader's huge house.

It appears from the various accounts that, despite the mob "in a state of frenzy," as Abd el-Kader described them, he and his men were not given any real trouble as they went about their rescue missions. The Algerians' reputation for having fought *jihad* in their home country still carried weight with the Muslims.

A few incidents stand out in the often confused descriptions of those days of violence. On one of his missions Abd el-Kader went to a Franciscan monastery and urged the monks to come with him. Afraid of treachery, they refused—only to die a little later when their house was torched by the mob. Another rescue attempt had a much better outcome. At an orphanage, fortunately outside the Christian quarter, the Sisters of Charity nuns and Lazarist fathers quickly marshaled their students, many barefoot but in uniform. Abd el-Kader and his sons, with armed Algerians on each side, led a procession of a few hundred children, plus the nuns and monks, to safety in the Emir's house.

What about the forces of law and order, while all this was going on? Abd el-Kader found no help from the religious leaders. When he hurried to the home of the mufti, early in the outbreak of violence, he was told firmly that the mufti was having his nap and could not be disturbed. Worse still, the Ottoman governor took no action. On that point, individuals who survived and described the riots were in total agreement. Some of the governor's soldiers joined in the looting and even turned their guns and bayonets on people trying to escape the fires. As the governor had warned Abd el-Kader, these troops were hardly the cream of the Ottoman army; but clearly, neither were they under any instructions to restore order. One Turkish commander who did try to stop the rioters was charged with insubordination.

THE COMPASSIONATE WARRIOR

For several nights Abd el-Kader slept on a mat at the entrance of his house, so that no one seeking refuge would be turned away. At dawn on the third day of the riots, July 11th, he confronted a large mob who knew that he was sheltering Christians and had come to his house demanding blood. According to the reports of this scene, the Emir stood before the men and waited until they finally quieted down. He appealed to the "law of God" and their own sense of humanity. Had they sunk so low in honor, he argued, that they wanted to slaughter defenseless women and children?

The mob still shouted for the Christians and even mocked Abd el-Kader, saying that he himself had been a "great killer of Christians."

"If I slew Christians," the Emir answered, "it was in accordance with law. They were invading our land and fighting against our faith. If you won't listen to me, then you are like beasts in the field, caring only for your food."

Still the crowd yelled for blood, until Abd el-Kader said, "These Christians are my guests. Try to take one of them, and you'll learn how well my soldiers fight. We will fight for a just cause, just as we did before!"[5]

He called for his horse and weapons. As he mounted, his men surrounded him, brandishing their own rifles and shouting *"Allahu akbar!* God is the greatest!" Intimidated, the mob gradually gave up and melted away. Abd el-Kader must have felt both relief and bitter disappointment, as he saw his threat of force win out over his appeal to reason and mercy.

TO THE CITADEL

All this while, Abd el-Kader's men kept patrolling the Christian quarter and bringing more people to his house. Although the refugees were now safe, they were suffering in the midsummer heat. Nobody kept track of numbers, but there may have been as many as four thousand men, women, and children by that time, packed into the Emir's house and courtyard without food and water, let alone sanitation. Abd el-Kader sent some to the homes of his brothers and friends, but conditions were still intolerable.

Finally he made a difficult decision: he appealed to Ahmad Pasha. The governor, by now fully aware of the horrors he had unleashed and the price he might personally have to pay later, offered to let the Christians come to the citadel. They would not be protected by Turkish soldiers, he promised, but by Abd el-Kader's Algerians.

The Christians, however, were horrified as the very thought of leaving their haven and begged Abd el-Kader not to send them out into the streets again. Abd el-Kader swore that he would defend them with his own life. Two of the consuls staying in the Emir's house volunteered to accompany the first group, and an armed Algerian guard was ready. Although many of the refugees still had to be dragged, they did reach the citadel in safety, and thereafter the Christians went with more confidence. Before long the citadel's large open courtyard was full of people, safe but suffering, as there was no shelter from the sun and very little food or water.

With his spacious house mostly emptied, Abd el-Kader went right back to rescuing more Christians. This time he used a different strategy, spreading word that anyone who brought a Christian refugee safely to his house would receive a monetary award. It worked, and for a few more days Abd el-Kader stayed close to his entrance, handing out coins to those who cooperated. Whenever a group of a hundred refugees had been gathered, they were taken to the citadel.

By the week's end, the fires of mass hysteria were burning out. The violent phase of this event—the worst sectarian conflict that Damascus or any other Arab city had experienced—was almost over. Accurate numbers of those killed could not be determined, but estimates of several thousand dead were probably reasonable, including people who later died of wounds and sickness. Unquestionably, the numbers would have been much, much higher without the efforts of Abd el-Kader and his Algerians. A common estimate is that eleven or twelve thousand Christians were saved in this way from almost certain death.[6]

The great majority of the Muslims of Damascus did *not* join in or approve of the riots. Earlier, many of the better educated Muslims had tried to dampen the rising tension. Now, horrified by the violence, they took in their Christian neighbors, often at risk to themselves. The massacre, fire, and destruction were actually confined to the Christian quarter, an area only about a third of a square mile. In another part of the city, where Christians lived as a minority among Muslims, there was little or no trouble, thanks to good leadership by Muslims and careful behavior on the Christians' part.

AFTERMATH

What became of the thousands of destitute refugees? The Christian quarter was totally destroyed—they had no homes left. Some people from the upper classes stayed for a while with Abd el-Kader and other Algerian families, or possibly with Christians in other parts of Damascus or in outlying villages. A great many people, however, had to remain for weeks in the citadel under grim conditions. Fortunately, the Turkish official in charge was a compassionate man and did the best he could.

Since there was no support for them in Damascus, many of the refugees set out for Beirut. At least three thousand, escorted in groups by Abd el-Kader's Algerians, crossed the two mountain ranges to the sea, most of them on foot. In Beirut, where foreign warships had arrived in response to the troubles in Mount Lebanon, they had a better chance of international attention and protection. Charitable groups such as American, British, and other missionaries could also offer some help, although their resources were already badly stretched by the thousands of refugees from Mount Lebanon.

As for the governor of Damascus, Ahmad Pasha, he was replaced with amazing speed. On July 16, 1860, just one week after the trouble started, the new governor arrived and tried to restore order. The situation remained extremely tense and dangerous.

By the second half of July, news of the riots and massacres had reached newspapers in Europe and the United States. The international reaction was quick. France and other European powers proposed to send a military force to Damascus—doubtless for reasons partly humanitarian but also plainly political. The Ottoman government knew that such an expedition would lead to further international pressures and even occupation, so they lost no time in planning a counter-move.

A highly respected Turkish diplomat, Fuad Pasha, had already been sent to deal with Mount Lebanon. By the time he got to Beirut, the trouble in Damascus presented him with an even bigger problem. On July 29th, accompanied by three thousand Ottoman soldiers, he entered Damascus with a show of force intended to convince both the people of Damascus and the international powers that he was completely in charge.

Fuad Pasha consulted efficiently with the European consuls and military officers, and also with Abd el-Kader. He then set up a special tribunal to arrest, try, and punish the perpetrators of violence—based largely on the memories of people who had experienced that violence. The tribunal made a list of some four thousand six hundred names and eventually narrowed it down to three hundred and fifty individuals, of whom three hundred and thirty-eight were found guilty. Not surprisingly, most of the one hundred and eighty-one executed by public hanging were from the lower classes, while the one hundred and fifty-seven more important individuals were sentenced to exile.

Ahmad Pasha, who had served as governor of Damascus for only a troubled six months, faced a firing squad. The extent and exact nature of his guilt is still somewhat uncertain; but whatever his actual role in the plot, clearly he did nothing to prevent or try to control the "murder, mayhem, pillage, and plunder."

As the fall season moved on, life slowly began to return to normal. The last refugees left the citadel in late September, and the Christian quarter was sufficiently cleaned up for rebuilding to start by January of 1861. Fuad Pasha also tried to deal with the immensely complicated matter of evaluating Christians' losses and determining compensation—while always on guard to prevent foreign criticism and intervention.

LOOKING BACK

How to explain such a vicious outbreak of sectarian violence in Damascus? Accusations flew in many directions. Plotting by the Ottomans? Or by either Great Britain or France, or both, to extend their political and economic influence in Syria? As for the Muslims, many of the violent looters were not residents of Damascus but came from outside, almost as if organized like a hired mob. In any case, rebelliousness, anger, and confusion were abroad in the land, just waiting to ignite.

And what about the Christians and their unwise behavior in a situation already very dangerous? The American vice-consul, Mishaqa, a Christian himself, pointed out that a minority with little power, living in a time and place of tension, should remember to defer to the powerful.

Abd el-Kader, too, took a serious view of the Christians' responsibility. They should have obeyed the law and paid their taxes, the relatively small amount that exempted them from military service. Even if the government is harsh, Abd el-Kader believed, the law must be obeyed. For government to function, authority must be respected and taxes paid. He knew the truth of that very well, from his own struggle to consolidate the Algerian tribes and create a new government.

ASSESSING ABD EL-KADER'S ROLE

Although other Muslims also rescued Christians in danger, Abd el-Kader played a unique and crucial role. He had tried repeatedly to warn the European consuls of the plot, and had warned Ahmad Pasha to stop before it was too late. He had mobilized his Algerians, urging them to encourage peace and tolerance, while at the same time preparing for the worst. He organized and directed a large-scale rescue mission day after day, venturing out in the dangerous streets and at times confronting the mob himself. He turned his own home into a refugee camp, not resting until thousands of desperate persons of all ages were as safely cared for as possible under extremely difficult conditions. His determination to keep going and to be wherever he was needed was like a reprise of his years as a resistance fighter in the countryside of Algeria.

Throughout Europe and the United States, the press and the public were as fascinated by reports of Abd el-Kader's role as they were horrified by the actual events. Now the image of the Emir as a protector of Christians overshadowed the vivid images of earlier years—first, the fierce opponent of Christian France, later the "desert hawk" unjustly imprisoned. The *New York Times* wrote: "It is no light thing for history to record that the most uncompromising soldier of Mohammedan [Muslim] independence . . . became the most intrepid guardian of Christian lives. . . ."[7]

THE COMPASSIONATE WARRIOR

The world saw Abd el-Kader as a hero almost without equal. He, however, saw his role in a different light. This is one of the most significant aspects of Abd el-Kader's actions in the Damascus riots. It was not desire for more fame that motivated him, or some form of reproach to the Ottomans, and certainly not a wish to gain still more favor from France. Rather, the Emir explained that he tried to save innocent lives because it was not only the morally right, humane thing to do, but the way to obey God's will. "These motives amounted to a sacred duty. I was simply an instrument," he said, as reported in the French press. In a personal letter he summed it up: "What we did for the Christians, we did to be faithful to Islamic law and out of respect for human rights."[8]

Nothing as extraordinary as Abd el-Kader's rescuing of the Christians, however, could have just one explanation. In spite of all he had said about putting political matters behind him, he remained a very perceptive political observer. He knew that attacks on the Christians of Syria would open the door to increased interference by European powers. Indeed, he had tried to get that warning across in the midst of the riots, shouting at the mob to think about what their "crazy behavior" would lead to. And he knew that if it came to open hostilities between the European powers and the Muslims of Syria, both the Turks and the local people, he would be caught in the middle. Abd el-Kader did not want to have a choice of that sort forced upon him.

There was another underlying reason. Abd el-Kader believed that Islam, the religion he followed so devoutly, needed to be restored and strengthened in the hearts of its believers. He wrote: "All the religions of the book [Islam, Christianity, and Judaism] rest on two principles— to praise God and to have compassion for his creatures. . . . The law of Mohammed places the greatest importance on compassion and mercy. . . . But those who belong to the religion of Mohammed have corrupted it, which is why they are now like lost sheep."[9] His own efforts, he must have hoped, could set an example of how a true Muslim lives his or her faith.

CHAPTER 12

ABD EL-KADER'S VISION FOR THE WORLD

When Abd el-Kader's efforts were no longer critically needed to help restore sanity in his adopted city, he withdrew from society. He needed time to cleanse his soul of the violence and madness in which he had been forced to immerse himself. For two months he lived at the Great Mosque of Damascus, praying, meditating, and healing. Someone from his house brought him one meal a day, his only contact with the outside world.

The Great Mosque was especially appropriate for Abd el-Kader's retreat. Built on the foundation of an early Christian church, which rested on much earlier pagan temples, it was completed in 715 C.E. by the earliest Muslim rulers of Damascus. On the walls were beautiful images of trees, gardens, rivers, and fountains, created in gold and brightly colored mosaics by Christian artisans from the Byzantine Empire. Water and lush greenery have traditionally been a powerful symbol of paradise for Muslims, but these images suggest something more: the possibilities of Christians and Muslims creating beauty and religious harmony together, a prospect dear to Abd el-Kader's heart.

THE COMPASSIONATE WARRIOR

Later in 1860, Abd el-Kader continued his spiritual revival by going on a short pilgrimage to an Islamic shrine in the Syrian city of Homs. On his return, he stopped at the famous Roman site in Baalbek, in what is now Lebanon. The temples and columns are still among the most enormous in the world, and it would be interesting to know what he thought as he marveled at the sheer size of those monuments to pagan gods. Could he see a connection between those religious ideas and his own?

HONORS AND MORE

While Abd el-Kader was trying to retreat from worldly concerns, the world was eager to shower him with honors. Napoleon III promptly sent him a medal for the highest honor that France could bestow, the Legion of Honor. Other countries followed suit, and medals came from Russia, Prussia, Greece, the Pope, and even the Ottoman sultan. In several of his photographs, Abd el-Kader displays all these large medals on a sash across his body. The American government sent him a pair of custom-made, gold-inlaid Colt pistols—a gesture that appears ironic at a time when the Emir was trying to put violence behind him.

Meanwhile, not content with medals, some people in France wished to honor the Emir by putting him back to work. In the fall of 1860, an anonymous pamphlet appeared in Paris, entitled "Abd el-Kader: Emperor of Arabia." The writer argued that the Ottoman Empire, on its last legs, should be replaced by an Arab empire made up of Syria, Mount Lebanon, Palestine, and part of what is now Iraq. Abd el-Kader would be the perfect head of state, the pamphlet stated, because of all his outstanding qualities and accomplishments. The proposal created quite a stir at first, but international rivalries soon put an end to it. If the French liked the prospect of Abd el-Kader ruling Syria, the British would inevitably block it—even though that meant continuing to prop up the Ottoman Empire.

CHAPTER 12: ABD EL-KADER'S VISION FOR THE WORLD

How did Abd el-Kader feel about the idea? No one, it seems, thought of asking him until a few months later. Then he made his wishes plain. "My career in politics is over. I have no ambition for worldly glory. From now on, I want only the sweet pleasures of family, prayer, and peace."[1]

In 1865, however, along came another job offer, this time from Napoleon III. He proposed that with the ever-increasing European settlement of Algeria, the country should be divided, one part for the Europeans, the other an Arab kingdom. And who for king better than Abd el-Kader? This idea never got off the ground. The European settlers were horrified, and Abd el-Kader was equally negative. Not only had he promised never to set foot on Algerian soil again, he said, but the Algerian people would not accept him. By now he was too progressive in outlook, too closely associated with aspects of modern thinking and western ways. The people of Algeria, impoverished and dispossessed, clung more fiercely than ever to traditional ways and would reject a leader who was now, in some respects, so different from them. Besides, he really meant it: he had no interest whatsoever in worldly power.

TRAVELS SACRED AND SECULAR

One trip, sacred in a way because especially dear to Abd el-Kader's heart, was very short. Every morning he carried his beloved mother Lalla Zohra up to the roof of his house, so she could sit in the sun. In 1861, at the end of a long life of both hardship and honor, deprivation and generosity, Lalla Zohra died. The loss struck deep in Abd el-Kader and contributed to his decision to undertake a third pilgrimage.

The Emir set out for Mecca on January of 1863. He wanted to make a double pilgrimage, requiring that he stay and take part in the pilgrimage of the following year. But while in Mecca, Abd el-Kader found himself so much in demand by Islamic scholars and other visitors that he had to retreat to his small room and live like a hermit. For months he studied and prayed, eating and sleeping so little that his health suffered. Recovering in time for the second pilgrimage, he returned to Damascus in June of 1864.

In the following year, Abd el-Kader undertook another trip, but of a very different sort: to Paris. This voyage, although one of his "secular" journeys, gave him a chance to demonstrate a spiritual value: his belief in reconciliation, even with wrong-doers. Stopping in Constantinople, he spoke directly with the sultan and asked for the release of the high-rank individuals from Damascus who, in the trials after the massacres, had been found guilty and exiled or imprisoned. Abd el-Kader was hardly a favorite in Constantinople, but his international renown and reputation for religious piety gave his arguments weight. The sultan listened and granted his request.

In France, enthusiastically welcomed by the Parisians, Abd el-Kader thanked Napoleon III in person for the honors he had received. He visited old friends, including his former interpreters Daumas and Boissonnet, went to the opera again, and attended a concert that demonstrated new musical instruments such as the saxophone.

Two years later, in 1867, back to Paris he went, officially invited to see the second Universal Exposition of science and technology. On this occasion Abd el-Kader also crossed the English Channel for the first time, to visit the country where he had aroused so much interest first as a resistance fighter, then as a "caged hawk," and finally as a protector of Christians. His four days in England, aside from an audience with Queen Victoria, passed simply enough. He enjoyed seeing the sights of London like any other visitor—Westminster Abbey, the British Museum, the Houses of Parliament—and especially the famous Crystal Palace, at that time the largest building ever made of plate glass. The latest achievements in technology were always high on the Emir's "must see" list.

CHAPTER 12: ABD EL-KADER'S VISION FOR THE WORLD

THE EMIR AND THE CANAL

The most important trip during this time in his life took Abd el-Kader to Port Said on the coast of Egypt, in the fall of 1869. The occasion was the opening of the Suez Canal, which linked the Mediterranean with the Red Sea. The celebration, which included the first performance at the elegant Cairo Opera House, built expressly for the occasion, was possibly the most splendid event of the century in the Mediterranean world. This was no casual visit for the Emir, or even a courtesy invitation to sit with dignitaries from all over Europe. He was particularly honored, because among all his other activities and interests, Abd el-Kader had played a key role in the construction of the canal.

Years earlier, while the Emir was still a prisoner in France, one of the prominent men who had visited him was the diplomat Ferdinand de Lesseps. Later, de Lesseps became the principal promoter for the canal project. Finding the ruler of Egypt reluctant to go along with the plan, in 1861 he visited Abd el-Kader in Damascus to ask for help. The Emir was delighted to become involved. He got busy writing letters, helped win the Egyptian ruler's approval, and the digging proceeded.

The whole Suez Canal project had a much more profound meaning for Abd el-Kader than just a triumph of modern engineering. This long-dreamed-of achievement now made it possible for ships to go from Europe to India and other points east without having to voyage all the way around Africa. Thus it was both a passageway and a bridge. It brought places closer together by connecting the great oceans and seas of the world; it linked East and West, along with the peoples and cultures of those worlds. Whether speaking to groups of engineers or the Canal Company's shareholders, Abd el-Kader always discussed the Suez Canal in spiritual terms, calling it "inspired by God." So important was the project to him in this sense, that on his return from his double pilgrimage to Mecca he made a point of stopping in Egypt at the construction site.

THE COMPASSIONATE WARRIOR

Connections and bridge-building, bringing different peoples in touch both physically and spiritually: that was what inspired Abd el-Kader most at this time in his life.

ABD EL-KADER'S IDEAS AND WRITINGS

Like his spiritual master, the medieval Sufi mystic Ibn Arabi, Abd el-Kader wrote abundantly. He started putting together his spiritual writings, many of which reflected the influence of Ibn Arabi, during his first years in Damascus. By conveying his spiritual and philosophical insights in writing, he carried forward the heritage he had received from studying the Sufi master in his youth. This vital connection is increasingly relevant today, as interest in Ibn Arabi is growing among scholars and in the Muslim world. The city of Ibn Arabi's birth in Spain, Murcia, holds a major international film festival in his honor each year, especially for films that emphasize conciliation, understanding, and respect for diverse beliefs.

The Emir's spiritual writings, based in Sufi mysticism, are difficult for most people to grasp; but for the purposes of this story of his life, one idea stands out clearly. Abd el-Kader firmly believed that God is a universal presence, the one enduring reality, and that all religions really worship the same God. Not just the three monotheistic Abrahamic religions (Judaism, Christianity, and Islam), but all others as well. He states: ". . . God addresses all those who have been reached by the Koranic revelation or earlier revelations—Jews, Christians, Mazdeans, idolaters, Manicheans and other groups professing varied opinions and beliefs with respect to Him—to teach them that their God is one. . . . All the beliefs which are professed about Him are for Him just different names."[2]

To further explain, he says: "Allah [the Arabic word for God] is not limited by what comes to your mind—that is to say, your creed—or enclosed in the doctrine you profess. . . . If you think and believe that He is what all the schools of Islam profess and believe—He is that, and He is other than that! If you think that He is what the diverse communities believe, He is that, and He is other than that! . . . Each of His creatures worships him and knows Him in a certain respect and is ignorant of Him in another respect."[3] In other words, says Abd el-Kader, no one religion or individual can know everything about God. Part of every understanding of God is true—but there's always more. God cannot be *completely* understood.

Abd el-Kader reminds his readers that the holy book of Islam, the Koran, explicitly states that differences are good, that God purposely created people to be different. Diversity of human communities, with differing cultures and religious ideas, is one of God's many blessings on humankind.

With these beliefs, Abd el-Kader could talk for hours with people who followed different religions—or no recognized religion at all. He could learn from them and share his own convictions, without having to insist that such-and-such a belief about God, or what God wanted, was absolutely right, or that a particular doctrine was wrong. The objective of dialogue was not to oppose or to win over, but to reveal the truths common to all religions.

Indeed, Abd el-Kader believed that his ability to accept "divisions" in understanding confirmed that he had a special role in bridging differences: Islam and Christianity, East and West. If both Muslims and Christians would listen to him, he said, it would prevent a lot of trouble.

"LETTER TO THE FRENCH"

A few years earlier, during his residence in Turkey, Abd el-Kader had set down his thoughts in quite a different way. A French scholar had asked him to write his autobiography, but the Emir chose to write

THE COMPASSIONATE WARRIOR

a long philosophical essay instead. It was published in Paris in 1858 and aroused much interest. Although Abd el-Kader gave it a different title, it has been known ever since as "Letter to the French"—meaning thoughtful persons of western society in general.[4] In contrast with the style of his spiritual writings, Abd el-Kader's "Letter" sounds as though he were talking to the reader. He points out truths about relations between people, and between humans and God, and suggests appropriate behavior. The Letter is his best known literary legacy. It is important today as a statement of ideas and faith by a Muslim who was traditionally educated and devout, but also remarkably open-minded and receptive.

The first section is about knowledge, both intellectual and spiritual. The second is on moral behavior, divine law, and the role of the prophets; and the third discusses the history and importance of writing.

In Abd el-Kader's view of the physical world, each animal and plant has a distinguishing characteristic that helps to define it. What makes humankind unique? The love of knowledge, the pursuit of truth. Desire for knowledge comes from a combination of intellectual and moral ability, which can perhaps best be referred to as *reason* (*aql* in Arabic). Abd el-Kader notes that reason differs from one person to another, both in "richness" and in quantity. Everyone has enough to acquire some knowledge, but some people have much more than others.

In discussing different kinds of knowledge, Abd el-Kader rather surprisingly puts *politics* at the most basic level—yet considers it the most important subject of knowledge. By "politics" he means simply the art of living together. Humans are social creatures and must cooperate in order to survive. Friction and quarrels are inevitable—between husband and wife, parents and children, shepherds and landowners, between *all* human individuals and groupings. Therefore, people need the kind of knowledge that guides behavior in a just and righteous way, based on generosity and caring rather than love of power. Religious

126

leaders should not seek power, he says, but they should oppose injustice and have the courage to confront the worldly rulers when those rulers are not wise or just.

Abd el-Kader greatly admired many things about France and especially the accomplishments of scholars and engineers. In his Letter he observes that it was the huge difference between modern knowledge and the stagnant traditional thinking of Algerian society that enabled France to conquer. He calls on the Islamic world to stop opposing progress under the guise of "preserving values and principles"; it should "liberate" knowledge, join modernity, and open itself to European knowledge—but control its own future.

Yet the Emir fears that modern society is too secular. French scholars are lacking in the spiritual realm, he believes, and should acknowledge God's role in their accomplishments. Without this recognition, people are not only ungrateful and cut off from divine wisdom, but headed for a fall.

Abd el-Kader's thoughts are clear on the persisting debate over science and intellectual knowledge versus faith. He sees no contradiction between them. Although faith is above reason, both are gifts from God. But using religion to deny science, and using science to deny religion, are both wrong.

Turning to moral improvement, Abd el-Kader says that along with *reason*, there are three other essential qualities. *Courage*, meaning moral courage, is the ability to do what is right with firmness, generosity, and compassion. Behavior based on *justice*, free from anger, greed, and envy, is the second quality. *Self-control* holds back destructive impulses. But *reason* is the most important quality, because it enables humans to tell truth from error, to have good judgment, and to approach divine wisdom.

The role of prophets has been to teach divine wisdom, or divine law. Abd el-Kader describes the prophets as "doctors of the spirit." Just as a good patient obeys the medical doctor, people should respond to the teachings of the prophets with faith and obedience.

But what if those teachings are hard to understand? Abd el-Kader tackles the difficult question of wealth in this context. It might be logical, he notes, to argue that a person should be allowed to keep all his wealth and use it only as he wishes. Reason, however, says something else. God created gold and silver, which have little use in themselves, to be utilized in exchange for things that are needed in life—food, shelter, clothing. Every person, the Emir says, needs and has a right to these basic things. Therefore, riches must be shared.

Generosity and neighborliness not only hold communities together but are at the core of all religions. Abd el-Kader reminds the reader that all the prophets of Judaism, Christianity, and Islam brought the same basic message: glorify God, and show compassion for all God's creatures.

An important point that Abd el-Kader makes with clarity: religious law is *not* fixed and permanent. Sticking blindly to "established opinion," he says, does not lead either to truth or to religious vitality. Just as a medical doctor may need to revise a prescription, religious law must change over time to meet changes in people's conditions and needs. After all, change—like all creation—comes from God.

In the third chapter of his Letter, Abd el-Kader discusses how the remarkable human accomplishment of *writing* developed through the achievements of the ancient Egyptians, Hebrews, Persians, Romans, and Greeks. He traces the path by which the works of the ancient philosophers—in Greek, Latin, Hebrew—were translated into Arabic by Muslim scholars during the height of Islamic civilization and later translated into European languages. Thus they were saved for world civilization. As he wrote this chapter, his thoughts must have returned to the loss of his own collection of precious manuscripts when his "floating capital," the *smala*, was destroyed.

These are some of the highlights of Abd el-Kader's ideas that he hoped would resonate with the educated people of the west.[5] "Letter to the French" is still of much interest today.

ABD EL-KADER AT HOME, WITH FRIENDS OF EVERY STRIPE

Whenever Abd el-Kader was at home in Damascus, steady streams of people came to see him—and he was rarely "too busy." For many a European traveler, a tour of the Middle East would have been incomplete without a visit to the Emir Abd el-Kader. He had gotten used to graciously receiving visitors during his days of imprisonment and as a free man in Paris; now he was able to keep up an even more welcoming style of hospitality. Although by this time he had learned some French, he preferred to speak in his own language, Arabic, with an interpreter at his side. It doesn't seem to have slowed down the conversation.

Occasionally Abd el-Kader must have surprised his visitors. An American traveler, who happened to be a dentist, visited the Emir and was startled when Abd el-Kader asked for a little dental work. The visitor said he would have considered it an honor, but he had not brought his instruments.

However firm his own religious and moral truths were, Abd el-Kader was always willing to embrace difference. Indeed he made sure that he would have plenty of opportunity, because his friends were certainly not all proper, or religiously upright, or even socially respectable people. He seems, in fact, to have been drawn especially to unconventional individuals. In the years following the troubles of 1860, two of Abd el-Kader's favorite visitors were among the most eccentric, controversial English personalities of their time.

Sir Richard Burton, the British consul in Damascus from 1869-71, was a man for whom no adventure was too risky. In disguise, he had actually visited Mecca on the pilgrimage—a feat strictly forbidden to non-Muslims. He knew twenty-five languages, had explored the source of the Nile River in Africa, and had wandered on horseback across South America. Enjoying his reputation as a "godless devil-of-a-fellow," he horrified people at dinner parties with lurid stories from his studies and travels. He and his wife Isabel spurned living in a fashionable house in the city and chose instead the shabby village of Salihiyya, where Ibn Arabi's tomb stood.

A thoroughgoing rebel, Burton rejected religious belief. In character, he was a man as different from Abd el-Kader as could possibly be—and the two became fast friends. With his wife Isabel—every bit his partner in exploring dangerous places, riding across the desert, shooting, and so forth—Burton spent many hours visiting with the Emir. When he was abruptly recalled from his job as consul, only two friends said goodbye as the Burtons left Damascus late at night—and one was Abd el-Kader.

The other was Jane Digby, a beautiful, intelligent, talented English woman. She and her husband—her fourth and favorite, an Arab Bedouin chief—lived six months each year in a tent in the desert. The other six months they lived in Damascus, where they frequently visited Abd el-Kader. Like Richard Burton, Jane Digby had long since rebelled against her aristocratic social class and for many years had made no secret of her constant search for love. As a mature woman, however, she was much more than just a charming eccentric. During the riots of 1860, she not only sheltered Christians but went into the smoldering

Christian quarter, its streets still strewn with corpses, to take food and medications to any survivors.

Isabel Burton's memoirs give quite a different picture of the Emir from the grave appearance in his many photographs. She describes how, when she and her husband visited, he would come forward "with outstretched hands to grasp mine, his face beaming," and soon serve cups of tea "with a peculiar herb."[6] Years later, she recalled the idyllic evenings spent on the roof of the Burtons' house with Abd el-Kader and Jane Digby. This unlikely foursome would smoke their narguilehs (elaborate water-pipes) and settle down to "talk and talk and talk far into the night, about things above, things on earth, and things under the earth. . . . It was all wild, romantic, and solemn."[7]

Abd el-Kader seems to have found so much to value in the friendship of both the Burtons and Jane Digby that ideas of socially correct behavior were quite irrelevant to him. With the rare gift of focusing on the essential qualities of the human being, he evidently felt free to associate with whomever he pleased, regardless of his own status in society.

Among Abd el-Kader's other close friends in Damascus was Dr. Michael Mishaqa, the American vice-consul who had so narrowly escaped death during the massacres. In his middle years, in Lebanon, he had abandoned his original Greek Catholic faith and accepted Protestantism, learned from American missionaries. He was well educated, thoughtful, and an esteemed medical doctor. In spite of his own act of religious rebellion, Mishaqa agreed with Abd el-Kader that public rebelliousness, as in the events of 1860, cannot be condoned. Deciding for oneself whether or not to obey authority, he believed, only leads to chaos.

There was one person whose relationship with Abd el-Kader had a special character because it had somehow withstood betrayal. That individual was Léon Roches, who had been so close to the Emir from 1837 to 1839 and finally admitted that he had never really accepted Islam. Roches, who later led a highly adventurous life as a secret agent and diplomat, kept in touch with Abd el-Kader through occasional correspondence. They exchanged sympathetic letters about the death of Abd el-Kader's mother, and when Roches was considering whether to write his memoir, Abd el-Kader encouraged him to do so.[8] Yet the two men were never to meet again face to face.

POLITICAL COMPLICATIONS—AND LINGERING QUESTIONS

Abd el-Kader lived for many years after the events of 1860 had focused the world's attention once more upon him. Even in his late years, however, he was not free of the political complications that had always bedeviled his life.

The Ottoman authorities viewed Abd el-Kader with intense distrust, all the more because of his loyalty to France. He had to walk a careful line between the two—the Ottoman Empire, growing weaker and therefore more harsh, and the French Empire, increasingly pushing into the Middle East and Africa. With the growing influences of Islamic revival movements and Arab nationalism, the Emir's relations with groups known to be hostile toward the Turks, such as the Druze and the religious brotherhoods, sharpened Ottoman suspicions. Yet, strangely enough, at least three of Abd el-Kader's close family members decided to support the Turks and became officials in Constantinople.

As for his continuing admiration and loyalty to France, it's hard to know just what to think of that extraordinary attachment to a former enemy. To be sure, Abd el-Kader depended on financial support from France, and a very large number of people depended on *him*. But considering the long sweep of his story, some questions persist. For instance, how could Abd el-Kader, recognizing that France intended to suppress his people completely and replace them with Europeans, have continued to respect his captors? How could he, knowing of the atrocities inflicted on his people by the French army, have been able to forgive and apparently forget?

There are no simple answers. Perhaps he did have that much power of forgiveness. Perhaps he was unusually capable of putting things behind him, closing the door on a major part of his past life, concentrating on the here and now—and of course, the eternal. He may have felt that his spiritual and mental health, and his ability to be a wise, clear-headed teacher and example to others, required that he avoid thinking about the condemnable behavior of his former enemy.

But the most important explanation may have lain in his complete trust in God. In December of 1847, at the time when Abd el-Kader decided to stop resisting, he was convinced that God had made the ultimate decision. God, the all-knowing and all-powerful, had determined that Algeria should henceforth be governed by France. Abd el-Kader's role, as a devout servant of God, was to accept the decision and make the best of it. Focusing only on the good qualities of the former enemy would logically be part of God's plan for him. In the end, Abd el-Kader's estimation of France may simply have to be accepted as part of the story of this infinitely complex, extraordinary man.

THE DESERT HAWK'S LAST YEARS

Aside from his awareness of what was going on in the world, Abd el-Kader's late years seem to have been comfortable and serene, surrounded by his family in his huge house in Damascus and his more restful house in the nearby countryside. For all his refusal of luxury, it is touching to note that the Emir did indulge himself in a few small ways. The traditional costume he wore was simple and unadorned but always of spotless white fabric, in contrast with his hair and beard—which remained very black. On occasion he might display his collection of medals, as when he sat for painted portraits by a variety of artists, and numerous photographs. At a time when even in Europe some people were still superstitious about their likenesses being "captured," Abd el-Kader was fascinated by photography.

It was always the *other* world, however, the one sought through prayer and meditation, that meant the most to Abd el-Kader. That world, close to his God, was what had always given his life its truest meaning. The end of that remarkable life came at the age of seventy-six after a short illness, on May 25, 1883.

Accompanied by respectful groups along the way, Abd el-Kader's body was borne from his country home the short distance to Damascus, in the carriage that Napoleon III had given him. The consuls and a large crowd were waiting to do him honor in the center of the old city, believed to be the ancient foundation of Damascus. From there he was carried to the Great Mosque for prayers. Finally, he was buried outside the city, next to the tomb of his spiritual master, Shaykh Ibn Arabi. He had chosen this resting-place even though it was in the rough, rundown area called Salihiyya, where the determined doubter Richard Burton had made his home. In death as in life, Abd el-Kader brought opposites together.

EPILOGUE:

ALGERIA AFTER ABD EL-KADER

The Emir Abd el-Kader kept his word and never returned to Algeria, yet he must have kept track of what was going on in his homeland.

LAST FLICKERS OF RESISTANCE

There were many years of terrible hardship and misery for the Algerian people when drought, crop failures, locust plagues, and epidemics brought famine and death. There were years of good harvest when the tribes could revive somewhat, only to be followed by another economic crisis. Occasional outbreaks of resistance to the French continued in the 1850s and 1860s, but any rebellion was soon crushed. Then the people would be punished, their villages and forests destroyed.

The last serious insurrection started early in 1871. Some eight hundred thousand people joined in, mostly impoverished Kabyles (Berbers), and for a few months attacked settlers' farms and villages and forts over a wide area. The French finished off the insurrection in June 1872, and this time imposed punishment intended to completely discourage any further thought of resistance. The tribes were all but ruined by land confiscation and financial penalties.

THE COMPASSIONATE WARRIOR

For several years the people of Algeria had one friend in a high place: the emperor of France. Napoleon III is a problematic figure in French history, criticized especially for his unwise foreign adventures. But where Algeria was concerned, he justified Abd el-Kader's faith in him. Calling for "perfect equality between natives and Europeans," including public education and access to civil and military employment, he promised his protection to the indigenous population. He wanted to stop the ongoing seizure of the Muslims' land and make Algeria a better country for everyone.

But Napoleon III's vision was doomed. In July of 1870, tensions in the European balance of power led France into a short but disastrous war with Prussia. The emperor was taken prisoner, the Second Empire met a swift end, and France became a republic once again.

Abd el-Kader's personal loyalty to Napoleon III never wavered. On one occasion not long after the French defeat, some visitors to his home were making sarcastic remarks about the disaster. After listening in silence, Abd el-Kader got up and left the room. He reappeared a few minutes later, now wearing the medal of the French Legion of Honor. It was a wordless statement of his continued esteem for the emperor who had bestowed it on him in 1860.

COLONIAL ALGERIA TRIUMPHANT

The settlers (*colons*) in Algeria were delighted with the outcome of the Franco-Prussian War. The military administration of the country was finished, and now the road was open to their complete control of Algeria. Coming from several Mediterranean and European countries in addition to France, the *colons* regarded themselves as quite distinct from Frenchmen. They were *Algerians*—in fact, the *only* Algerians. The indigenous Arab and Berber people were referred to simply as Muslims, and they existed, just barely, on the margins.

Meanwhile, the relationship of Algeria to France had been made even more complicated by one of the strangest political arrangements ever thought up by a colonial power. In 1848, the government of the Second Republic had declared Algeria an actual part of France—not a colony or a possession, but as much a part of the mother country as Brittany or Provence or Paris itself. It meant, at least in theory, that the laws and policies of France would apply equally to Algeria. The *colons*, however, vigorously resisted any action from Paris that did not please them.

The new "Algerians" dealt with the native population in three main ways. Seizing more and more of the Muslims' land by whatever means possible, they pushed the rural people into ever smaller, more arid, less productive areas. Second, their representatives in the French Parliament made it official policy to undermine Muslim society and identity. The traditional aristocracy lost all power. The marabouts, Abd el-Kader's class, were given a somewhat protected status, but lost the people's respect because regarded as collaborators. The Islamic judicial system was restricted almost out of existence.

The third line of attack consisted of humiliating and discriminatory measures. The Muslim population was subjected to prosecution and punishment in ways never applied to the Europeans, and forced to pay heavy taxes imposed exclusively on them. In short, the *colons* intended to reduce the Muslims to a permanent and powerless underclass, a source of cheap labor and nothing more.

There were many people in France who deplored this gross injustice. Certain statesmen and administrators tried persistently to bring about reform, but the settler society and government of Algeria could always block any change that might affect their total domination of the country.

THE COMPASSIONATE WARRIOR

THE "CIVILIZING MISSION" OF FRANCE

What about the renowned French civilization, so much admired by Abd el-Kader? From the very start of the conquest, some observers had called for spreading this civilization to the conquered people through education. But how? For the entire history of French Algeria, one approach after another was tried, with little or no success. In any case it hardly mattered. The *colon* communities refused everything that would benefit the Muslims.

For many years the indigenous people themselves were reluctant to accept the schools offered by their conquerors. After World War I, however, when many Algerian Muslims served in the French army, people began to see the need for modern education. Suddenly the demand for schooling took off—but the schools were not there. By the 1950s, on the eve of drastic change in Algeria, the indigenous people were still 85-90% illiterate, and for women the estimate was as high as 98%. The very few urban Muslims who had managed to receive secondary and higher education did not include professions that would be needed for a modern nation. The French "civilizing mission" in Algeria was always a matter of much too little, much too late.

Nevertheless, lack of education did not stop Algerian Muslims from starting to work for reform. The early activists, in the 1920s, included former soldiers who had seen something of Europe, urban workers, and men who had gone to France for work. They found ways to organize, mostly underground, and called for civil, political, and human rights equal with the European population.

ABD EL-KADER'S NATIONALIST HERITAGE

Did the Emir Abd el-Kader, who had fought so hard for freedom a century earlier, leave a personal heritage that could contribute to the future struggle? His large family of brothers and ten sons, did not follow in his footsteps. His grandson Khaled, however, became one of the first Muslims who could be called an Algerian nationalist.

In 1919, Khaled presented a petition to the American president, Woodrow Wilson, calling for justice toward the Algerian Muslims. A few years later, with a military education and career behind him, Khaled became a prominent voice for reforms such as equal status and greater political representation. He was elected to public office, wrote a weekly paper called "Audacity," and bothered the *colon* government enough for them to send him into exile. Khaled attempted to keep up the struggle by connecting with political groups in Paris, but was caught, imprisoned, and again exiled. Like his grandfather he was sent to Damascus, where he died in 1936; but his reputation continued to influence the growing nationalist organizations.

The Emir Abd el-Kader's importance as a national symbol would come later.

ALGERIA'S WAR FOR INDEPENDENCE

The North African campaign of the Allies during World War II, especially the American military landing in November 1942, brought international attention to Algeria. One of the most prominent nationalist leaders, Ferhat Abbas, drew up a manifesto in 1943 calling for an autonomous Algerian state, still connected to France. A year later, General Charles de Gaulle, president of the Free French government in exile, signed a decree abolishing all discrimination against Muslims. But again, it was too little, too late. Most of the nationalist leaders by then wanted a free Algerian state. After ten years of frustration, even the moderate Ferhat Abbas had to admit that "There is no other solution than the machine gun."[1]

On November 1, 1954, a series of terrorist actions in Algeria and a formal declaration announced the start of the Algerian war for independence. The primary organization coordinating the struggle, the FLN (National Liberation Front), were ready to negotiate with the French government if it recognized the Algerian Muslims' rights to self-determination, but the answer was "No." French Algeria, still regarded as an integral part of the mother country, would be defended by every means possible.

The Algerian war grew into the longest, most destructive, bitter, and bloody of any of the struggles for self-determination following World War II. It not only devastated the land of Algeria, but led to violent crises in the French homeland and within the French army. By March 1962, France finally realized that military victory was impossible and Algeria was lost.

With an independent Algeria established, almost the entire European population packed their bags and left. With them went most of the managers, merchants, professionals—in short, the people needed to run a modern state. It was something like the exodus of the Turkish ruling class in 1830, which left the French conquerors facing an ungovernable country.

Fortunately, the modern Algerian nationalists had foreseen the need for organization. Much as Abd el-Kader had tried desperately to organize his people, army, and state under constant threat of war, the nationalists had to learn how to manage in the midst of conflict. While perhaps inevitably, independence for Algeria has been marked by dissension and disappointment, the free nation has withstood severe threats and has succeeded as a fully functioning, vigorous member of the international community.

One of the first ceremonial acts of the new government was to bring the great national hero, the Emir Abd el-Kader, home at last. In 1966 his remains were transported from the tomb in the foothills above Damascus and reinterred in the cemetery of Algiers. A fitting gesture—but not without irony. Abd el-Kader's own wishes had been to remain for eternity in Damascus, next to his spiritual guide Ibn Arabi.

ABD EL-KADER IN HIS OWN TIME AND TODAY

The Emir Abd el-Kader—young, handsome, and vigorous at the start of his struggle, noble and astonishingly able throughout his career—was a true international celebrity. In the nineteenth century many books and articles were written about him as a resistance-leader and as the embodiment of interfaith good will. For the French and others who knew him, including people of the Arab and Muslim worlds, he was a hero of the highest order. In 1873 the *New York Times* summed up his career thus: "If to be an ardent patriot, a soldier whose genius is unquestioned and whose honor is stainless, a statesman who could weld the wild tribes of Africa into a formidable army, and a hero who could accept defeat and disaster without a murmur—if to be all these constitutes a great man, Abd-el-Kader deserves to be ranked among the foremost of the few great men of the century."[2]

Although his fame had dwindled by the middle of the twentieth century and few people unfamiliar with North Africa knew about him, today Abd el-Kader is again starting to receive the attention he deserves. His story is highly appropriate for our times, when we need understanding and cooperation among followers of the world's religious faiths more than ever.

It seems right, moreover, that Abd el-Kader should be remembered as one who faithfully tried to carry out *jihad*—in its most authentic sense of struggle for righteousness and in the most meaningful ways. Just as he fought against the oppression of his own people, he fought against wrongdoing that afflicted others. Throughout his life, he tried to combat injustice and narrow-minded ignorance. And perhaps most valuably for today, he encouraged the spiritual and moral meeting of minds, the shared path of mutual respect by which all humans may walk toward truth.

NOTES

CHAPTER 1: BARBARY PIRATES AND FRENCH ADVENTURES

[1] Pierre Genty de Bussy, *De l'Établissement des Français dans la Régence d'Alger* (Paris: Firmin Didot Fréres, 1839), p. 202.

CHAPTER 2: AN UNLIKELY LEADER EMERGES

[1] Bruno Étienne, *Abdelkader* (Paris: Hachette/Pluriel, 2010), p. 109.

CHAPTER 3: THE EMIR'S STRATEGY

[1] Mahfoud Bennoune, *The Making of Contemporary Algeria, 1830-1987* (Cambridge, UK: Cambridge University Press, 1988), p. 38.

CHAPTER 4: ABD EL-KADER'S VISION FOR HIS PEOPLE

[1] Raphael Danziger, *Abd al-Qadir and the Algerians: Resistance to the French and Internal Consolidation* (New York: Holmes & Meier, 1977), p. 95.

CHAPTER 5: FRENCHMEN IN THE EMIR'S LIFE

[1] Ahmed Bouyerdene, *Emir Abd el-Kader: Hero and Saint of Islam* (Bloomington, IN: World Wisdom, 2012), p. 53.

CHAPTER 6: WAR OF TOTAL CONQUEST

[1] Bruno Étienne, *Abdelkader*, p. 176.

CHAPTER 7: THE DEVASTATING TIDES OF WAR

[1] Rachel Heavner, ed., "Abd-el-Kader in British and American Literature," *CELAAN* (*Review of the Center for the Studies of the Literatures and Arts of North Africa*), Vol. 6, Nos. 1 & 2, Spring 2008, pp. 58-59.

CHAPTER 8: PROMISES KEPT AND BROKEN

[1] John W. Kiser, *Commander of the Faithful: The Life and Times of Emir Abd el-Kader* (Rhinebeck, NY: Monkfish Book Publishing, 2008), p. 210. Many travelers in the

nineteenth century kept detailed diaries and journals, as well as writing long letters to friends and family. Naturally most of those who met the Emir would have wanted to do the occasion justice. Thanks to the popularity of writing, along with the Emir's own letters to officials and friends, we have an interesting record of his speech and behavior, plus insights into his thinking and emotions.

[2] Wilfred Blunt, *Desert Hawk: Abd el Kader and the French Conquest of Algeria* (London: Methuen, 1947), p. 234.

[3] Ibid., p. 235.

[4] John Kiser, *Commander of the Faithful*, p. 217.

[5] Ibid., p. 217.

[6] Wilfred Blunt, *Desert Hawk*, p. 238.

CHAPTER 9: THE IMPRISONED CELEBRITY

[1] John Kiser, *Commander of the Faithful*, p. 229.

[2] Wilfred Blunt, *Desert Hawk*, p. 240.

[3] Ibid., pp. 231-32.

[4] *CELAAN*, p. 45.

[5] Ibid., p. 51.

[6] Wilfred Blunt, *Desert Hawk*, p. 245.

[7] Ibid., p. 247.

[8] *CELAAN*, p. 23.

CHAPTER 10: FREEDOM AND A NEW LIFE IN EXILE

[1] Vista Clayton, *The Phantom Caravan, or Abd El Kader, Emir of Algeria* (Hicksville, NY: Exposition Press, 1975), p. 262.

[2] John Kiser, *Commander of the Faithful*, p. 255.

[3] Ahmed Bouyerdene, *Emir Abd el-Kader*, p. 138.

[4] Wilfred Blunt, *Desert Hawk*, p. 256.

[5] John Kiser, *Commander of the Faithful*, p. 262.

CHAPTER 11: MADNESS IN DAMASCUS

[1] Ahmed Bouyerdene, *Emir Abd el-Kader*, p. 108.

[2] Vista Clayton, *The Phantom Caravan*, p. 283.

[3] Ahmed Bouyerdene, *Emir Abd el-Kader*, p. 111.

[4] "The Damascus Massacres: Letter from Abd-el-Kader," *The New York Times* archive, August 20, 1860.

[5] Because Abd el-Kader spoke in Arabic, which was then usually translated into French and later into English, it is impossible to have completely accurate records of what he said. This is true for the quotations attributed to him throughout this book. In this particular scene of confrontation—at which no one was taking notes, of course!—we can have only the gist of what was said. The dialogue appears in three or four different books, all varying slightly but agreeing on the general ideas.

[6] Leila Tarazi Fawaz, *An Occasion for War: Civil Conflict in Lebanon and Damascus in 1860* (Berkeley: University of California Press, 1994), p. 97.

[7] "Abd-el-Kader and the United States," *The New York Times* archive, October 20, 1860.

[8] John Kiser, *Commander of the Faithful*, p. 302.

[9] Ibid.

CHAPTER 12: ABD EL-KADER'S VISION FOR THE WORLD

[1] John Kiser, *Commander of the Faithful*, p. 311.

[2] Michel Chodkiewicz, *The Spiritual Wriings of Amir 'Abd al-Kader* (Albany, NY: State University of New York Press, 1995), p. 125.

[3] Ibid., pp. 127-28.

[4] Abd el-Kader's original title suggests how he regarded the purpose of his essay. He called it (translated from the Arabic): "Brief Notes Intended for Those with Understanding in Order to Draw Attention to Essential Questions." That was shortened

somewhat to the following: "Reminder to the Intelligent, Advice to the Indifferent."

[5] In addition to Abd el-Kader's *Lettre aux Français* (Algiers: Editions ANEP, n.d.) itself, this discussion is based mainly on treatment of the subject in John Kiser, *Commander of the Faithful*, pp. 265-72 and Ahmed Bouyerdene, *Emir Abd el-Kader*, pp. 125-26, 136, 144, 180, 193.

[6] Isabel Burton, *The Inner Life of Syria, Palestine, and the Holy Land* (London: Henry S. King, 1875), p. 125.

[7] Isabel Burton and W. H. Wilkins, *The Romance of Isabel Lady Burton*, Vol. 2 (London: Hutchinson, 1897), p. 397.

[8] Léon Roches' autobiography, *Trente-deux ans à travers l'Islam*, published in Paris in 1887, was written some forty-five years after the time he spent with Abd el-Kader. Although he relied on personal letters and other documents from the period, that time-lapse—and his tendency to romanticize—should be kept in mind. Nevertheless, his descriptions are among the most detailed and vivid of the many reports written about the Emir.

EPILOGUE: ALGERIA AFTER ABD EL-KADER

[1] Charles-Robert Ageron, *Modern Algeria: A History from 1830 to the Present* (Trenton, NJ: Africa World Press, 1991), p. 106.

[2] *The New York Times*, February 25, 1873, in *CELAAN*, p. 101.

TIMELINE

1807: Abd el-Kader, son of Muhyi ad-Din and Lalla Zohra, is born in Guetna near Mascara.

1825: Abd el-Kader and his father leave for the pilgrimage (*hajj*) to Mecca; imprisoned in Oran by Turkish bey for about a year.

1827: Return from pilgrimage, having also visited to Egypt, Syria, and Iraq.

1830: France conquers Algiers in retaliation for dey's insult to the French consul; start of the French conquest of Algeria.

1832: Muhyi ad-Din leads *jihad*—resistance—against French in western Algeria; Abd el-Kader active in attacks on Oran. Tribal leaders accept Muhyi ad-Din's proposal of his son as leader; Abd el-Kader recognized as "Commander (*amir*) of the Faithful."

1833: Abd el-Kader consolidates his power in western Algeria. Death of Muhyi ad-Din.

1834: Abd el-Kader and General Desmichels sign treaty, enlarging territory under the Emir's control.

1835: Desmichels recalled; French step up war on tribes. Abd el-Kader's army soundly defeats French at battle of Macta River.

1836: French defeat Emir's army at Sikkak River, but fail to take Constantine in eastern Algeria.

1837: Abd el-Kader signs a second treaty, with General Bugeaud; Treaty of Tafna further enlarges Emir's territory. French army conquers Constantine.

1838: Abd el-Kader overcomes the fortress of Ain Madhi in the Sahara by siege. The Emir's army at its greatest strength.

1839: New French governor-general, Valée, breaks Treaty of Tafna. Abd el-Kader resumes combat, attacking European settlements.

1841: War intensifies under Bugeaud as governor-general. French take most cities. Emir proposes and achieves prisoner exchange with the help of Christian clerics.

1842: Abd el-Kader establishes the *smala*, a tent city, as his "floating capital."

1843: Duke of Aumale destroys the *smala*; Emir, army, and remains of his camp retreat to Morocco for safety.

1844: Morocco drawn into conflict with France; sultan now regards Abd el-Kader as enemy.

1845: Insurrections led by Bou Maza and others. French kill many civilians trapped in caves. Abd el-Kader's guerilla warfare revives. French military expedition destroyed at Sidi Brahim, prisoners held in Abd el-Kader's camp.

1846: French prisoners killed at camp. Abd el-Kader retreats to Morocco again.

1847: With army and tribal support weakened, Abd el-Kader comes under attack by both Moroccans and French; moves his camp back to Algeria. In December Abd el-Kader decides to stop fighting, approaches French general. His terms accepted, with family and followers he is transported to Toulon, France.

1848: French government breaks promise, imprisons Abd el-Kader and his Algerians first in Toulon, then Chateau of Pau in Pyrenees, then in Chateau of Amboise near Paris. Political changes in France: abdication of King Louis-Philippe, declaration of Second Republic, election of Louis-Napoleon Bonaparte as president. By law, Algeria declared part of France.

1849: Continuing controversy over whether to release Abd el-Kader because of distrust and suspicions regarding killing of French prisoners. Support for Abd el-Kader from many individuals.

1851: Louis-Napoleon declares himself prince-president in bloodless seizure of power.

1852: Louis-Napoleon liberates Abd el-Kader, who then visits Paris as honored guest. France becomes an empire, with Louis-Napoleon now called Emperor Napoleon III. Abd el-Kader, his family, and followers embark for exile.

1853: Contrary to original agreement, Abd el-Kader and Algerians exiled to the heart of Ottoman Empire; settles in Bursa, Turkey.

1854: Crimean War (France, Great Britain, and Ottoman Empire fight against Russia).

1855: Abd el-Kader goes to Paris, requests change of residence; Napoleon III agrees. With family and followers, the Emir journeys from Turkey to Damascus. He settles down as honored teacher of religion and head of Algerian community.

1856: Crimean War concludes with allies' victory; peace terms forced on the Ottomans regarding the rights of Christians foreshadow trouble.

1857: Abd el-Kader makes pilgrimage to Holy Land (Jerusalem, Bethlehem, Hebron).

1858: Publication of Abd el-Kader's "Letter to the French" in Paris.

1860: Severe sectarian conflict in Mount Lebanon. Abd el-Kader tries to prevent possible attack on Christians of Damascus, prepares for trouble. Riots and massacres break out; the Emir and his Algerians rescue and save lives of many Christians. Abd el-Kader honored by European nations and the United States.

1861: Death of Abd el-Kader's beloved mother, Lalla Zohra.

1863: Abd el-Kader undertakes double pilgrimage to Mecca.

1864: Returns to Damascus, visiting construction site of Suez Canal en route from Arabia.

1865: Abd el-Kader visits Paris. In Constantinople, requests release of individuals found guilty following 1860 massacres.

1867: Abd el-Kader's last visit to Paris at the invitation of Napoleon III; enjoys Universal Exposition of industrial and technological achievement. Briefly visits London and meets Queen Victoria.

1869: He attends official inauguration of Suez Canal; honored for his earlier support of the canal project.

1870: France defeated in war with Prussia; Second Empire ends; Third Republic (1870-1940) proclaimed.

1871: Last significant uprising in Algeria; French impose severe punishment on tribes. Rise of European settler (*colon*) power.

1883: Death of Abd el-Kader at his home near Damascus; burial near tomb of his spiritual master, medieval Sufi thinker Shaykh Ibn Arabi.

GLOSSARY

agha (Turkish): an administrative officer, next in importance to a *khalifa*.

Allah (Arabic): literally, "God"; the name used by Muslims and Arabic-speaking Christians to refer to the one God.

baraka (Arabic): "blessing" or "protection"; believed to be sent by God.

bey (Turkish): title of a provincial governor under the Regency of Algiers.

burnous (Arabic): a hooded cloak, usually of wool.

colon (French): a settler; a member of a colony established by one country in the territory of another country.

consul: official representative of a government, stationed in another country.

corsair: a privateer; a sea-going raider working on behalf of his government.

dey (Turkish): supreme ruler of the Regency of Algiers, under the Ottoman Empire.

emir (Arabic *amir*): "commander," "prince"; Abd el-Kader's title was "Commander of the Faithful."

Druze: a religious sect related to Islam, centered in parts of Lebanon and Syria; the word can be used for the religion and for the members, both single and plural.

Greek Catholic: a form of Christianity under the pope of Rome, following rites different from those of Roman Catholicism.

Greek Orthodox: a form of Christianity under the patriarch of Constantinople, following rites different from those of Roman Catholicism.

guerilla warfare: irregular combat, such as rapid, unexpected attacks, harassment, and sabotage by small groups of fighters.

hajj (Arabic): the pilgrimage to Mecca; persons who have made the pilgrimage can be called *hajj* or *hajji*, a term of respect.

indigenous: original, or native, to a certain locality.

Islam (Arabic): literally, "submission" (to God's will); the religion founded by the prophet Muhammad in the seventh century C.E. in Arabia, based on belief in one all-powerful and all-merciful God.

jihad (Arabic): literally, "struggle"—primarily moral and spiritual, but also to protect Islam and Muslims against assault.

khalifa (Arabic): "lieutenant," "second-in-command," representative of the commander.

khan (Arabic): a large building, usually in a town, where caravans could stop on their trading routes.

Koran (Arabic): the holy book of Islam, consisting of revelations that Muslims believe were delivered from God to the prophet Muhammad; also spelled *Qur'an*.

makhzen (Arabic): the "warrior" tribes used for tax-collecting and control under the Regency of Algiers.

marabout (Arabic *marbut*): a member of the religious and intellectual elite of traditional North African society, esteemed for their piety and possible supernatural powers.

Maronites: followers of a form of Christianity related to Roman Catholicism; the largest Christian group living in Mount Lebanon.

mosque: an Islamic house of worship, equivalent to a church or synagogue.

mufti (Arabic): a high Islamic official who interprets the religious law for Muslims.

Muslim (Arabic): a follower of Islam; also spelled "Moslem." (The word "Mohammedan" is obsolete and *not* acceptable.)

narguileh: a form of pipe for smoking tobacco—the smoke is cooled by passing through water in a special bottle; also called a water-pipe or "hubbly-bubbly."

orthodox: the form of a religion or other thought system recognized as established or "correct."

Ottoman: the Turkish empire that originated in Central Asia and spread westwards by conquest, establishing its capital in Constantinople in 1463 and controlling the Arab lands of southwest Asia and North Africa, along with the Balkans and parts of Eastern Europe; defeated in World War I, it soon afterward ceased to exist.

pasha (Turkish): a man of high rank and importance, originally under the Ottoman Empire.

pilgrimage: a journey to visit a certain place for religious reasons; the pilgrimage to Mecca, the birthplace of the prophet Muhammad and the holiest site in Islam, is a duty required of every Muslim, if at all possible.

pitched battle: a battle in which plans are laid and forces arranged in advance of actual combat.

qadi (Arabic): an Islamic judge.

Qadiriyya (Arabic): the religious brotherhood to which Abd el-Kader belonged; founded in medieval times by Abd al-Qadir al-Jilani ("Qadir" is another spelling of "Kader").

qaid (Arabic): an administrative officer at the tribal level.

Ramadan (Arabic): the month in the Islamic year during which Muslims fast from dawn to twilight as a religious duty.

rayah (Arabic): the settled agricultural and nomadic tribes in traditional Algeria, with less power than the *makhzen* tribes.

THE COMPASSIONATE WARRIOR

regency: a form of "semi-royal" rule; the name given to the whole territory of Algeria under the Ottoman Empire.

republic: a form of government with a non-royal chief of state who usually shares power with a group of representatives of the people, selected by popular vote.

royalist: pertaining to rule by a hereditary monarch.

sectarian: pertaining to the coexistence of two or more different sects—or religious groups—living in a certain place.

shaykh (Arabic): a chief of a subdivision within a tribe; also a spiritual master of a Sufi order.

smala (Arabic): literally "household"; the name given to Abd el-Kader's "floating capital," a tent city for tens of thousands of military and civilian residents.

spahi (Turkish): a member of a cavalry corps of indigenous Algerians serving in the French army.

Sufism: a mystical form of Islam that emphasizes devotional exercises aimed at bringing the Sufi close to God.

sultan (Arabic): supreme ruler; title of the head of the Ottoman Empire.

tribe: a large group held together by family ties and a strong sense of identity.

zawiya (Arabic): a religious (Sufi) center, traditionally including places for instruction, study, and prayer plus living quarters for students and scholars; akin to a monastery.

zouave (Berber): a member of an infantry corps of indigenous Algerians serving in the French army.

SELECTED BIBLIOGRAPHY

Two books were particularly useful in my research for this biography: *Commander of the Faithful: The Life and Times of Emir Abd el-Kader*, by John W. Kiser, provides a vivid, detailed account of the long era of combat between the Algerians and the French conquerors, as well as the Emir's later life. For emphasis on the spiritual side of Abd el-Kader and its contribution to his worldly role, I found many helpful insights in Ahmed Bouyerdene's book, *Emir Abd el-Kader: Hero and Saint of Islam*.

Abd el-Kader. *Lettre aux Français*. Algiers: Editions ANEP, n.d.

Ageron, Charles-Robert. *Modern Algeria: A History from 1830 to the Present*. Trenton, NJ: Africa World Press, 1991.

Arquilla, John. *Insurgents, Raiders, and Bandits: How Masters of Irregular Warfare Have Shaped Our World*. Chicago: Ivan R. Dee, 2011.

Bennoune, Mahfoud. *The Making of Contemporary Algeria, 1830-1987*. Cambridge, UK: Cambridge University Press, 1988.

Blunt, Wilfrid. *Desert Hawk: Abd el Kader and the French Conquest of Algeria*. London: Methuen, 1947.

Bouyerdene, Ahmed. *Emir Abd el-Kader: Hero and Saint of Islam*. Translated by Gustavo Polit. Bloomington, IN: World Wisdom, 2012.

Burton, Isabel. *The Inner Life of Syria, Palestine, and the Holy Land*. London: Henry S. King, 1875.

Chodkiewicz, Michel. *The Spiritual Writings of Amir 'Abd al-Kader*. Albany: State University of New York, 1995.

Clayton, Vista. *The Phantom Caravan, or Abd El Kader, Emir of Algeria*. Hicksville, NY: Exposition Press, 1975.

Danziger, Raphael. *Abd al-Qadir and the Algerians: Resistance to the French and Internal Consolidation*. New York: Holmes & Meier, 1977.

Daumas, Eugène. *The Horses of the Sahara*. Translated by Sheila M.

Ohlendorf. Austin, TX: University of Texas, 1968.

———. *The Ways of the Desert.* Translated by Sheila M. Ohlendorf. Austin, TX: University of Texas, 1971.

Djebar, Assia. *Fantasia: An Algerian Cavalcade.* Porstmouth, NH.: Heinemann, 1993.

Étienne, Bruno. *Abdelkader.* Paris: Hachette/Pluriel, 2010.

Fawaz, Leila Tarazi. *An Occasion for War: Civil Conflict in Lebanon and Damascus in 1860.* Berkeley: University of California Press, 1994.

Harik, Elsa Marston. "The Civilizing Mission of France in Algeria: The Schooling of a Native Population." In *The Politics of Education in Colonial Algeria and Kenya,* by Elsa Marston Harik and Donald G. Shilling. Athens: Ohio University Center for International Studies, 1984.

Heavner, Rachel, ed. *Abd-el-Kader in British and American Literature.* Review of the Center for the Studies of the Literatures and Arts of North Africa (CELAAN), Vol. 6, Numbers 1 & 2, Spring 2008, Saratoga Springs, NY, Skidmore College.

Kiser, John W. *Commander of the Faithful: The Life and Times of Emir Abd el-Kader.* Rhinebeck, NY: Monkfish Book Publishing, 2008.

Koulakssis, Ahmed, and Gilbert Meynier. *L'Émir Khaled, premier za'im? Identité algérienne et colonialisme français.* Paris: L'Harmattan, 1987.

Mishaqa, Mikhayil. *Murder, Mayhem, Pillage, and Plunder: The History of the Lebanon in the 18th and 19th Centuries.* Translated by Wheeler M. Thackston, Jr. Albany: State University of New York Press, 1988.

Ruedy, John. *Modern Algeria: The Origins and Development of a Nation.* Bloomington, IN: Indiana University, 2005.

Sullivan, Antony Thrall. *Thomas-Robert Bugeaud: France and Algeria, 1784-1849: Politics, Power, and the Good Society.* Hamden, CT: Archon Books, 1983.

Wolf, John B. *The Barbary Coast: Algiers Under the Turks 1500 to 1830.* New York: W. S. Norton, 1979.

BIOGRAPHICAL NOTES

ELSA MARSTON is an award-winning author of over 20 teen and children's books, specializing in the Middle East and North Africa, ancient and modern. She has a master's degree in international affairs from Harvard University with further study at the American University of Beirut, and has lived in Egypt, Lebanon, and Tunisia with her husband, the late Professor Iliya Harik of Indiana University. In addition to her books with Wisdom Tales (*The Compassionate Warrior* and *The Olive Tree*), her recent work includes *Santa Claus in Baghdad and Other Stories About Teens in the Arab World*, *Women in the Middle East: Tradition and Change*, *The Byzantine Empire*, and *Muhammad of Mecca*, a historical biography. She lives in Bloomington, Indiana.

BARBARA PETZEN is Director, Middle East Connections, and sits on the board of directors of the Abd el-Kader Education Project. She previously served as outreach coordinator at the Harvard Center for Middle Eastern Studies. She has designed and taught courses on Middle Eastern history, Islam, and women's studies at Dalhousie University and St. Mary's  University in Nova Scotia, Canada. She earned degrees from Columbia College and Oxford University, which she attended as a Rhodes Scholar. Her academic interests include the history and present concerns of women in the Middle East and the Islamic world, the role of Islam in Middle Eastern and other societies, relations and perceptions between the Islamic world and the West, and the necessity for globalizing K-12 education in the United States.

INDEX

Teachers, educators, parents, and students can visit:
www.wisdomtalespress.com
for free educational materials, including study
guides and discussion questions, to facilitate the use
of this book in classroom and independent study.

Personal wax seal of Abd el-Kader

For more information and an array of resources
about Emir Abd el-Kader, please visit the
Abd el-Kader Education Project website:
www.abdelkaderproject.org
Started in Elkader, Iowa, the Abd el-Kader
Education Project is growing a worldwide
movement to revive the legacy of Emir Abd el-
Kader. Their goal is to restore the historical
memory of a remarkable human being whose
importance today is greater than ever.